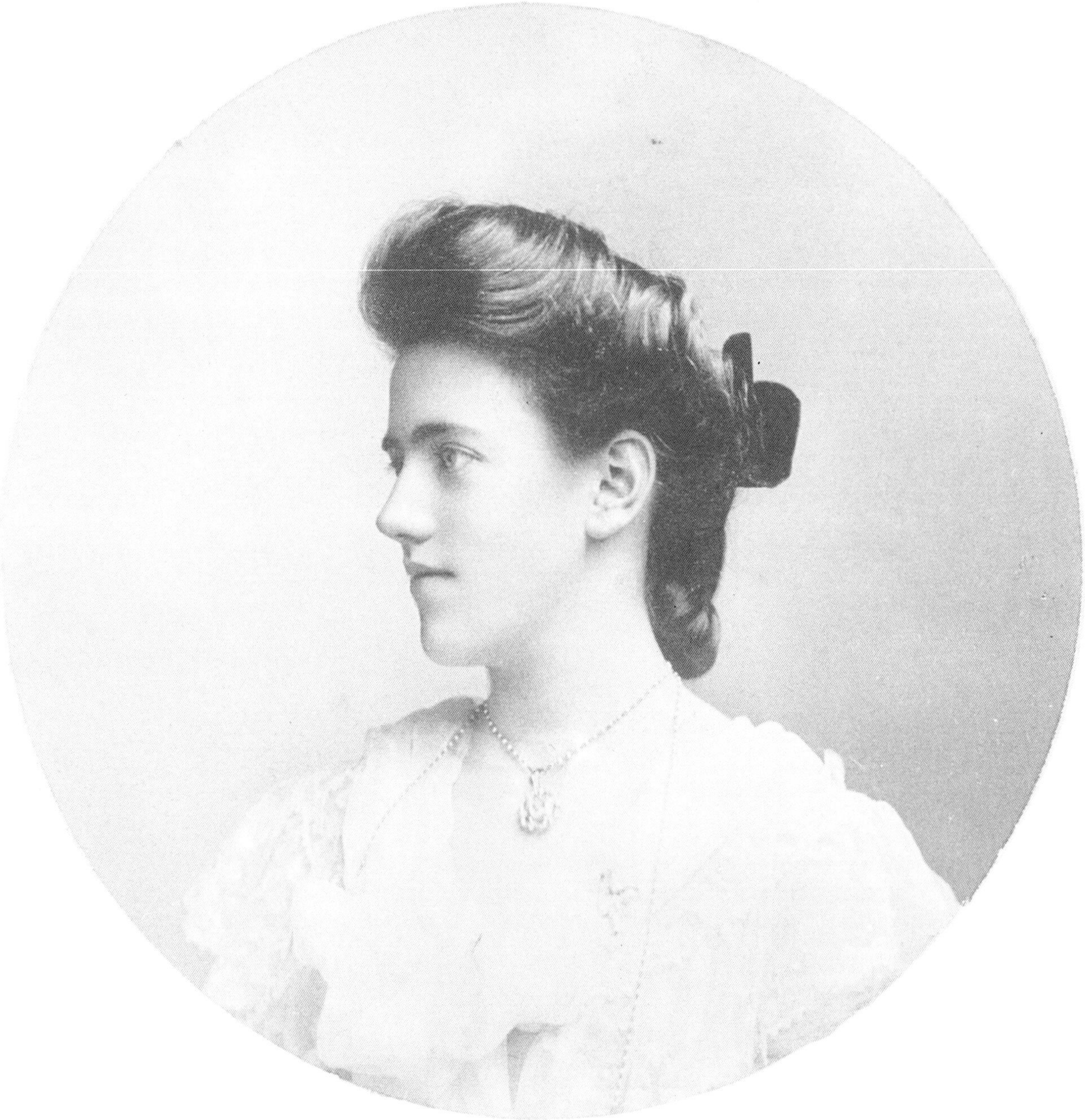

GWENDOLINE DAVIES

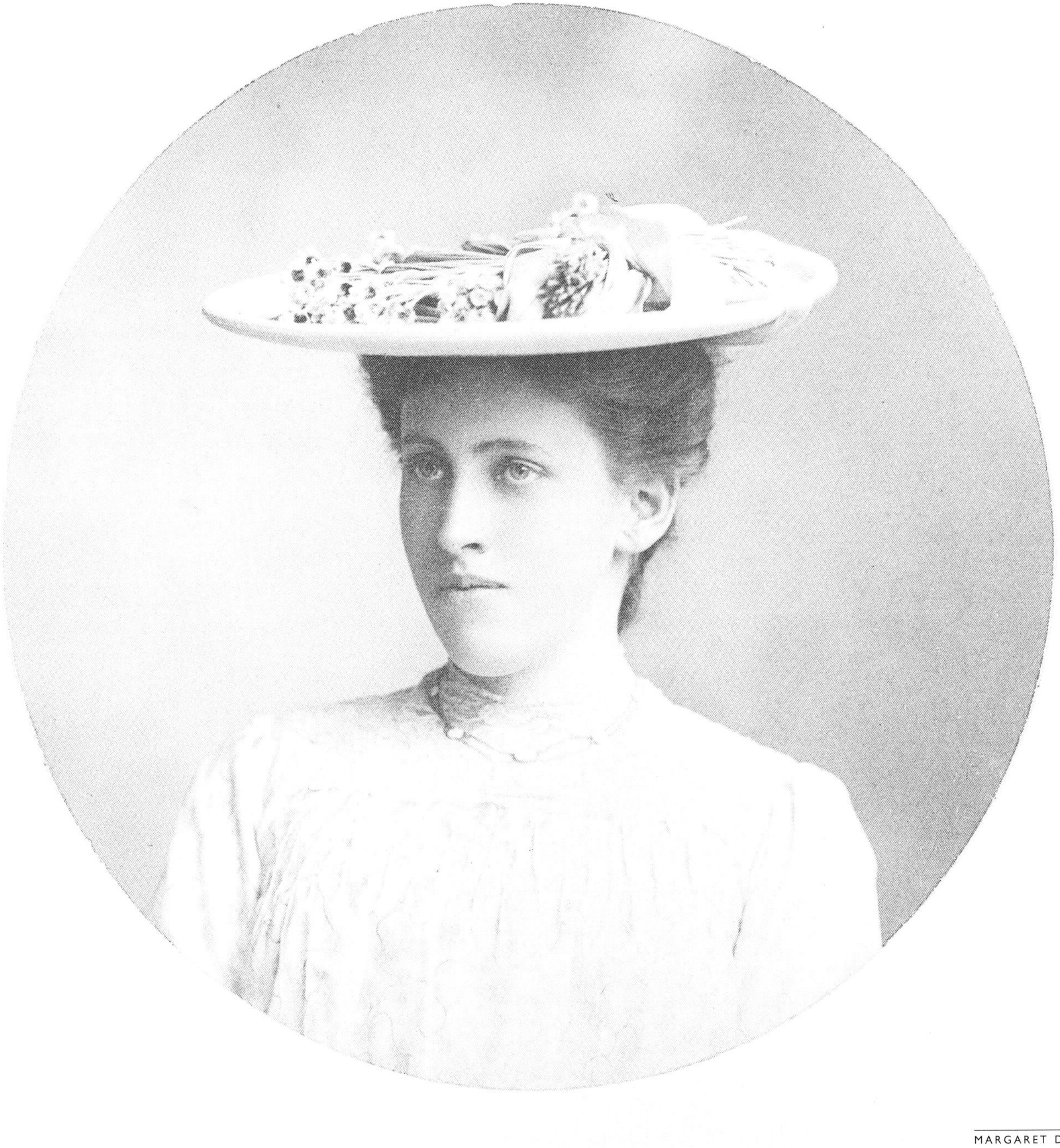

MARGARET DAVIES

First published in Great Britain in 2000 by the National Museums & Galleries of Wales, Cathays Park, Cardiff CF10 3NP

On the occasion of the exhibition
Sisters Select: works on paper from the Davies collection
National Museum & Gallery, Cardiff, 30 September 2000 – 11 February 2001
School of Art, Aberystwyth, 19 March 2001 – 18 May 2001
Victoria Art Gallery, Bath, 25 August 2001 – 4 November 2001

ISBN: 0 7200 0490 X

British Library Cataloguing-in-Publication Data
A catalogue record for this book is available from the British Library.

Design and production by A1 Design, Cardiff
Printed in Wales by MWL Print Group Ltd

CONTENTS

FOREWORD

Although the National Museums and Galleries of Wales has had many generous benefactors since its foundation in 1907, the sisters Gwendoline and Margaret Davies occupy a unique place in our history. During the First World War they were major donors to the National Museum's building fund, while their personal collections of paintings and sculpture, bequeathed to the National Museum of Wales in 1952 and 1963, transformed the range and quality of our art collections. The French 19th-century oil paintings and sculptures given by the sisters are now internationally renowned and are regularly requested for loan to major exhibitions around the world. However, the drawings and watercolours they also gave are less well known.

The sisters purchased many of these works already framed and did not themselves distinguish between them and their oil paintings as museum curators do today, though they were aware of the damage caused to works on paper by exposure to daylight. Today these works are stored in the National Museum and Gallery's Prints and Drawings Study Room and their display is carefully controlled. This exhibition in our changing programme is the first time that this part of the Davies collection has been shown. This is also the first publication to examine this aspect of the collection. The major role that Hugh Blaker played in the formation of the collection is acknowledged here but their independence and individual taste also emerge.

Any study of the Davies collection owes a great debt to the work of John Ingamells, whose book on the collection of French art, published in 1967, remains an invaluable work of reference. This publication builds upon his pioneering study and on the research of Robert Meyrick, Senior Lecturer and Keeper at Aberystwyth School of Art whose studies of Hugh Blaker and of the Gregynog collection of prints have been so enlightening. We also pay tribute to the research of Mark Evans, Head of Paintings at the Victoria and Albert Museum and formerly Assistant Keeper at the National Museum and Gallery. Dr Evans's knowledge of the Davies collection is unique and he has worked with Ann Sumner and Oliver Fairclough on the editing of this publication. The idea for the exhibition came from Assistant Curator (Prints and Drawings) Bethany McIntyre, who has worked tirelessly to meet tight deadlines, and has written a stimulating account of this aspect of the collection. Others who have given of their time and expertise include Jon Bennington of the Victoria Art Gallery in Bath where the Davies Collection was displayed from 1918 to 1920, Sue Sloman, David Hill and Tom Mulhearn, Director of Gregynog. All members of the Art Department have contributed to the exhibition but especial mention must be made of the conservators for the works on paper, Emily Gilbert and Christine Mackay.

We are particularly grateful to the Friends of the National Museums and Galleries of Wales. Their generous support has made possible a publication which does justice to this little-known facet of the Davies collection. Our Publications Department oversaw its design and production against tight deadlines, and again we thank all those concerned.

Anna Southall Director, National Museums & Galleries of Wales
Michael Tooby Director, National Museum & Gallery

GWENDOLINE AND MARGARET DAVIES – COLLECTORS OF WORKS ON PAPER

The story of Gwendoline Davies (1882-1951) and Margaret Davies (1884-1963) is a remarkable one: two spinster sisters brought up in mid Wales, with no family tradition of art collecting, who amassed one of the great British art collections of the twentieth century. In 1951 and 1963 they bequeathed two hundred and sixty works to the National Museum of Wales, transforming its art collection in character, quality and range. Seventy-four of these works form their important collection of works on paper. It is this aspect of their collecting which is examined in this study.

The sisters' first recorded purchase of a work of art was a watercolour drawing, *An Algerian* by Hercules Brabazon Brabazon,[1] which Margaret purchased in 1906 from an exhibition at the Goupil Gallery, London.[2] They continued to build up an extensive collection of works on paper which has been overshadowed, until now, by their collection of paintings and sculptures. Gwendoline bequeathed thirty-one works on paper to the National Museum of Wales and Margaret, the more prolific collector, forty-three. As would be expected, they acquired some important 19th-century French drawings and watercolours with fine examples of the work of Paul Cézanne, Honoré Daumier, Pierre Puvis de Chavannes, Paul Signac and Camille Pissarro. They also purchased 18th and 19th-century British work, including watercolours and drawings by J.M.W. Turner and William Blake (*see Plate 6*) as well as 20th-century examples by Augustus John, Josef Herman, Oskar Kokoschka, Stanley Spencer, Percy Wyndham Lewis, Frank Brangwyn, Eric Gill, J.D. Innes and Ray Howard Jones.

FAMILY BACKGROUND

Gwendoline and Margaret Davies were the granddaughters of David Davies of Llandinam (1818-1890) a man who from humble beginnings as a sawyer, amassed a fortune from contracting, coal-owning and the development of railways and docks. Their mother Margaret Jones died prematurely in 1888 and their father, Edward Davies (1852-98) then married her sister Elizabeth Jones (1853-1942). In 1898 Edward Davies also died and Margaret, Gwendoline and their brother David (1880-1944)[3] were brought up by their stepmother Elizabeth at Plas Dinam, in a strict Calvinistic Methodist tradition.[4] Their faith was to have a profound influence on Margaret and Gwendoline, who remained teetotal and were strict sabbatarians throughout their lives. Although their upbringing forbade such activities as dancing and the opera, both developed an early interest in the arts. Margaret sang, played the harp and briefly attended the Slade School of Art, and Gwendoline was a competent musician, playing both the violin and the organ. Both sisters travelled abroad widely, accompanied by their governess Jane Blaker.

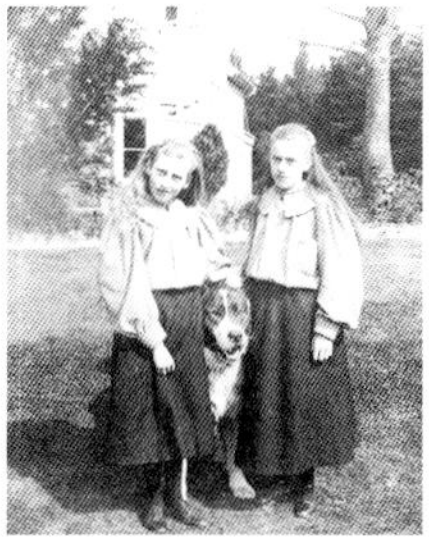

Gwendoline and Margaret Davies at Plas Dinam

By 1907 the two sisters were among the wealthiest unmarried women in Britain, with a joint fortune of around £1,000,000 and an annual income of approximately £40,000 in the boom years preceding the First World War.[5]

They continued the philanthrophic family tradition, supporting causes such as the campaign against tuberculosis. By 1908 they were also spending a considerable amount of their income on forming an art collection.

Gwendoline and Margaret's joint overall expenditure on watercolours and drawings is much less than that on oil paintings and sculpture. They frequently spent over £3000 per work on oil paintings, but all the watercolours and drawings cost less than £1000 each with the exception of a Turner watercolour of *Ehrenbreitstein* (now re-identified as *Würzburg*), purchased in 1919 for £1520. The French works were still relatively inexpensive. For example, a year after buying *Würzburg*, Gwendoline purchased two Cézanne watercolours for £165 each and in 1922 purchased two Daumier drawings, *Head of a Man* and *Two Studies for Return of the Prodigal Son* for £200. Watercolours and drawings are generally less expensive than oil paintings, but the lower overall expenditure is also due to the smaller number of works on paper purchased. The acquisitions of watercolours and drawings only exceeded those of oil paintings in one year, 1919, when Gwendoline purchased a large group of works by Augustus John.

Both Gwendoline and Margaret started to collect avidly in 1908. They jointly spent over £19,000 in this year on six oil paintings and one watercolour, a view of Rye in Sussex by Turner (*see Plate 8*), which they bought for £682.10.0 from Christie's. This purchase is the first of many instances when Hugh Blaker (1873-1936) acted on behalf on the sisters.

ADVISORS AND DEALERS

At different stages the sisters relied on a number of people for help and advice regarding their collection. Gwendoline wrote in 1923, 'We have at our call: Blaker, Maynard, Urquhart, Fred Richards[6], Greenslade[7] & lots of others.'[8] Of all these it was Blaker who played the biggest part in the formation of their collection. They were introduced to Hugh Blaker by their governess, Jane Blaker, who was his sister. At different stages in his career Blaker was an artist, writer, critic, collector, connoisseur and Curator of the Holburne of Menstrie Museum in Bath (1906-1913). He probably introduced the sisters to collecting whilst he was working in Bath, subsequently becoming their advisor and agent. Following the Davies bequest to the National Museum of Wales Murray Urquhart (1880-1972) wrote, 'so much is due to Blaker, indeed everything is due to him'[9]. He was indispensable in many of their purchases and guided the sisters toward collecting French art, including watercolours and drawings. He also kept the sisters informed of interesting works he had acquired himself. He wrote to Gwendoline in 1918, 'I have a beautiful Turner water colour of Cologne - one of the series of Rhine Drawings of 1819… I think it would be very cheap at £450 or so. The subject is the quay with a number of figures and boats and buildings in the mist. This is just a report of my latest acquisition in case you or Miss Daisy[10] would be interested before it is sent to America… Hope I don't appear "pushful": it is simply a notification of a very fine series - many have fetched very large prices. I think Thomson would want about a thousand for it! You once intimated that I should let you know when I have anything of interest so I venture.'[11] In fact, Gwendoline did not

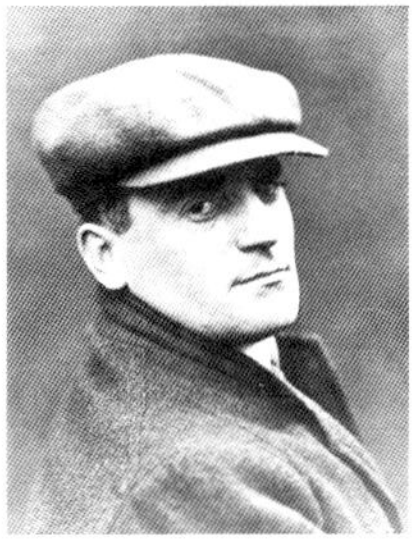

Hugh Blaker

purchase the watercolour until 1919 via the Barbizon House Gallery for £350. Although Blaker considered himself to be their main advisor, he was never the architect of the collection. Gwendoline wrote, 'The great joy of collecting anything is to do it yourself - wth expert opinion granted, but one does like to choose for oneself, all the time we have been collecting our pictures we have never bought one without either having seen it or at least a photograph before purchasing.'[12]

Eager to put the collection on display, Blaker initiated loans to public galleries. In February to May 1913 an exhibition of loan works was held at the City Hall, Cardiff under the auspices of the National Museum of Wales, and later at the Holburne of Menstrie Museum, Bath.[13] In 1918 he corresponded with his friend John Witcombe[14] (1872-1918), Curator of the Victoria Art Gallery, Bath, regarding the loan of some works.[15] Many of works lent, including two paintings by Cézanne, arrived directly from the Bernheim-Jeune Gallery in Paris, being exhibited in Britain for the first time. This highly innovative exhibition received over 5000 visitors in 19 days and necessitated Sunday afternoon openings.[16] It caught the interest of the national press and of critics and artists such as Clive Bell. No works on paper were exhibited in the 1913 exhibition and only one, Augustus John's *Pyramus John*[17], was included in the 1918 exhibition. This suggests that at this time works on paper were purchased more for private enjoyment than public exhibition.[18]

Murray Urquhart, a life-long school friend of David Davies, became a close friend of Blaker and the sisters. He assisted with the management of the collection, particularly after Blaker's death in 1936, and was the driving force behind the 1913 exhibition.[19] Robert Ashwin Maynard (1888-1966), who became the first Controller of the Gregynog Press in 1921, also became an advisor and aide to the Davies sisters.[20] He managed the conservation of the works of paper in the collection.

Having been introduced to the art world by Blaker and others, the sisters began to purchase directly from galleries. David Croal Thomson of Wallis & Son sold them many works in the early years of their collecting. He wrote to Gwendoline on 18th July 1910, 'Given the lines you have set yourself you will soon have a first rate collection'.[21] The anticipation of a great collection already existed. The sisters also became acquainted with Emile Bernheim.[22] He corresponded frequently with the sisters in French regarding works he had available in his gallery, Bernheim-Jeune, in Paris, and visited them in London. Having purchased the Cézanne paintings from him both sisters went on to buy other works, including many of their French 19th-century watercolours. In comparison with his flamboyant partners, Emile Bernheim was a modest man who rode his bike to work, which probably appealed to the sisters' sense of restraint.[23]

EARLY COLLECTING

Margaret and Gwendoline collected both jointly and independently and it was only possible to determine the exact ownership of the works in retrospect. Curators at the time were also sometimes unaware of what each sister owned. In a letter to one of the sisters (probably Gwendoline) thanking her for their loan of works to Bath, dated April 24th 1918, John Witcombe wrote: 'I do not know if I ought to include your sister in these thanks. I mean I do not know the precise ownership of the various works. I feel sure I ought, so will you be so kind as to ask her to accept this very inadequate acknowledgement.'[24] Even though many purchases appear to have been a joint venture, an assessment of the watercolours and drawings in the two bequests reveals that both sisters had purchased according to their own distinctive tastes and aims.

GWENDOLINE'S COLLECTING

Between 1908 and 1923 Gwendoline acquired thirty-one works on paper by five different artists. Modern scholarship distinguishes works on paper from paintings; however, at the time both Gwendoline and Margaret purchased watercolours and drawings alongside their purchases of oil paintings. They were not building a separate works on paper collection.[25] For example, Gwendoline made her first purchase of a watercolour, *Rye, Sussex* by Turner (see *Plate 8*), in the same year as purchasing the oil painting *Morning after the Storm*, in 1908. By the end of 1913 she had purchased three more watercolours by Turner, but had also started to acquire continental 19th-century works including her first continental works on paper: a watercolour by Daumier entitled *The Lawyer and his Client* (see *Plate 4*) and the Symbolist work, *Joyous Walk* by Matthuis Maris.

In September 1916 Blaker noted in his diary that he had 'inspired the Davies girls' to buy Rodin's *Eve* and 'some early John paintings and two drawings'.[26] Gwendoline had purchased ten oil paintings by Augustus John and one drawing, an image of his son Pyramus. Three years later she purchased ten more drawings (see *Plate 12*) and a set of etchings. Hugh Blaker was an ardent supporter of John's work. After the artist was rejected by the army in 1916, Blaker wrote, 'Genius is too rare stuff for German machine guns, and I rejoice'.[27] Blaker was particularly interested in John's drawings, writing an article on them for *Colour*. On meeting John for the first time he encouraged him to photograph a preliminary drawing for a thirty-nine foot decoration for the Arts & Crafts show at the Royal Academy, as 'the drawing is so vital and 'big'.[28] Gwendoline collected more works on paper by John than by any other artist. He was an excellent draughtsman, so it was logical to represent John in their collection with figure drawings as well as oil paintings.

Having purchased two oil paintings by Cézanne in 1917, Gwendoline added three of his watercolours three years later. Only two of these are now in the National Museum & Gallery, *The Diver* and *The Bathers* (see *Plate 1*). The other, *Nature Morte*, was sold by Margaret at Sotheby's in 1960. This is the only work purchased by Gwendoline to be sold and was probably a joint acquisition. In the same year she also purchased a watercolour by Signac, *St Tropez*, from the Eldar Gallery. Brightly coloured landscapes are a theme that recurs throughout the sisters' collection. This work and the Cézanne watercolours are finished compositions and although watercolours, would have been considered, framed and hung in much the same way as the oil paintings.

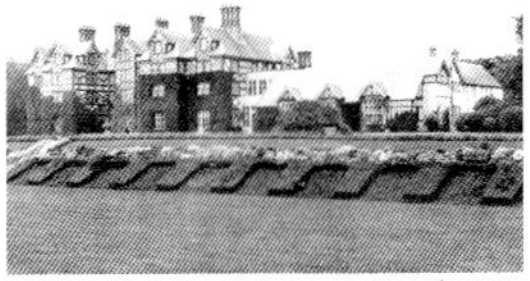

Gregynog Hall

Between 1921 and 1923 the only works on paper which Gwendoline bought were three by Daumier, *The Lawyer Walking*, *The Head of a Man* and *Two Studies for The Return of the Prodigal Son.* Aside from a few oil paintings these were the last purchases she made. This decline in activity is explained in a letter she wrote, dated November 1921, to Thomas Jones (1870-1955), then Assistant Secretary to the Cabinet, editor of *The Welsh Outlook* and a close friend and advisor to the sisters, which states: 'Thank you for telling us about the John pictures. I have not bought any for 18 months, we simply cannot in face of the appalling need everywhere - Russian children, Earl Haig's ex-soldiers, all so terribly human. After all, it is humanity that needs help and sympathy isn't it?'[29]

By this time Gwendoline was preoccupied with other matters. Not only was she supporting a growing number of social causes, but she was becoming increasingly involved with the development of Gregynog, a house and estate near Newtown which the sisters purchased in 1920, as a centre for artistic development in Wales. The sisters moved there in 1924 and it remained their home until 1960 when Margaret gave it to the University of Wales as a centre for educational use. This move would have also meant the sisters had less hanging space for their collection.

In 1952 Gwendoline bequeathed all her artworks of national importance to the National Museum of Wales.[30] Margaret compiled a list of the works which Gwendoline owned. The Museum's Director and Keeper of Art decided all thirty-one works on paper offered were of national importance and they were therefore accepted.

MARGARET'S COLLECTING

Margaret was a much more prolific collector of works on paper. Forty-three drawings and watercolours came to the National Museum from her bequest, though she owned others. Margaret was able to draw herself and was probably more attracted to drawings and watercolours than her sister. In the early years, Margaret only purchased two watercolours, *An Algerian* by Brabazon in 1906 and *Return from the Fields* by Israëls in 1910. By 1912, when the pace of their collecting had increased and they had begun to make important purchases of French 19th-century works, Margaret was acquiring some fine British and European works on paper. These included Léon Lhermitte, *The Return of the Harvesters* (see *Plate 3*), two Turner watercolours, *St. Goar* and *Forest Road,* and two works by George Clausen, *West Door of the Parthenon by Moonlight* and *The Saw Pit.* In March 1914 Margaret purchased Jan Hendrik van Mastenbroek, *Canal at Overschie, Setting Sun.* She ceased purchasing works on paper until 1920, when in the space of one year she made twelve important purchases: *Study for 'Legende de Ste Geneviève'* by Puvis de Chavannes, four Maurice de Vlaminck watercolours, six drawings by Pissarro (see *Plate 2*) and a Turner watercolour, *Falls of the Rhine.* This was the same year Gwendoline purchased the two Cézanne watercolours and the Signac.

From 1921-1927 Margaret turned her attention to the work of British artists. She purchased a portrait of *Ezra Pound* (see *Plate 9*) by Percy Wyndham Lewis in 1921, five watercolours by Alfred Rich in 1923 and a Turner landscape, entitled *Landscape with Cattle*. This overriding and diverse interest in British art proved typical of her later collecting.

After a gap of 7 years Margaret resumed collecting in 1934, but with a different aim and emphasis. The works from this period are of a quite different character. Margaret moved away from the prevailing French influence of the early years and concentrated on British 20th-century art. She continued acquiring in this vein until the last months of her life. Although she spent significantly less on the works during this second phase, her purchases were regular and plentiful. During this time she bought a group of 18th-century topographical views of Wales by Moses Griffith (*see Plate 7*), but the majority were drawings and watercolours by artists such as Augustus John, JD Innes, Murray Urquhart, John Piper, Paul Nash, Josef Herman (*see Plate 10*) and Stanley Spencer. She acquired representative works of modern art and rarely purchased more than one work by each artist. She also began to visit and purchase from different galleries, and the exhibitions of the Royal Society of Watercolour Painters, the Fine Art Society and the South Wales Group.

The impetus for Margaret's resumed collecting was due to a number of factors. She was a trained artist,[31] which may have influenced her decision to purchase works by her contemporaries, but was also interested in advancing the standard of art produced in Wales. She may have been collecting good examples by contemporary artists to encourage this aim. Both Margaret and Gwendoline had been present at the inaugural meeting of the Contemporary Art Society of Wales in 1937 and served as officers. Margaret became Vice President, having been proposed by the Executive committee as the first President but deferring in honour of Augustus John. She also acted as their purchaser in 1954.[32] This was a reflection of her innate interest in contemporary art and a stimulus for her own collecting. Many of the French artists whose work Gwendoline and Margaret had purchased some thirty years earlier were by now highly regarded and accepted in Britain and their instinct had proved prophetic. It is possible that Margaret was purchasing with this same thought in mind, or felt that the collection as a whole would be more complete if brought up to the present.

Margaret sold seven works at Sotheby's on 24th February 1960 and a further eighteen works on 4th May for a total sum of £48,870. These included some important watercolours and drawings by Millet[33], Vlaminck, Pissarro, Turner, Daumier and Cézanne. The artists were all well represented in the collection and the money from the sales was redirected to further purchases of predominantly modern works. Margaret lent many of her paintings to the National Museum in this year and consulted John Steegman, Keeper of Art, about her collection. It was generally assumed that the collection was destined for the Museum. He wrote to Margaret, 'This means that the collection must now be considered as having passed from the private to the institutional stage. If that is accepted… the personal tastes or distastes of the collector must to some extent give way to the tastes and requirements of the art-interested public, … not only of today but also of tomorrow.'[34] He urged her to 'round off' her collection with some semi-abstract works or examples of modern Expressionist Schools. Some of her last purchases, such as a Kokoschka watercolour, *Landscape with Bonfire,* were sent directly to the Museum.

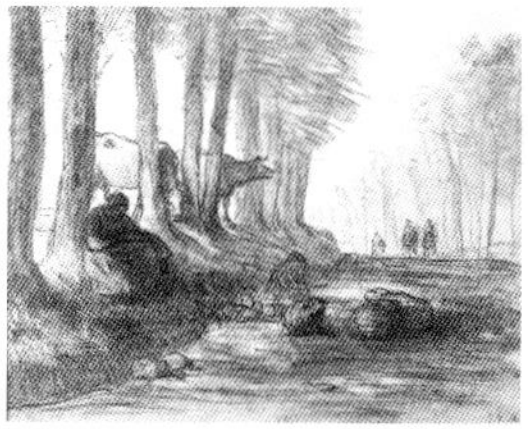

Jean François Millet, On the Roadside, *sold at auction in 1960. Whereabouts unknown.*

Margaret was making the final purchases of what was about to be a national, rather than a personal, collection. As her will reaffirms, she was aware of the distinction of her later purchases and intended that her modern paintings should tour to a wide audience. In 1963 forty-two watercolours and drawings came to the National Museum of Wales as part of Margaret's bequest of works of national importance[35], twenty-one from the second period of collecting.

Although most of the works in Margaret's collection, excluding those works bequeathed directly to the University of Wales, were acquired by the National Museum, there were many other drawings and watercolours at Gregynog. They were offered for sale to the University of Wales in accordance with Margaret's will. The majority of them are still at Gregynog or on loan to the School of Art, Aberystwyth. They are mainly watercolours, drawings and prints by friends and acquaintances, those who knew the sisters or those who stayed at Gregynog such as Charles Sims, Murray Urquhart, Hugh Blaker, the Belgian artists George Minne and Valerius de Saedeleer, together with some of Margaret Davies' own works.

Gwendoline and Margaret also acquired prints. These included a set of eighty-four Augustus John etchings, five works by Albrecht Dürer, three by Rembrandt, *The Thames Set* of etchings by James Whistler, five works by Jean-Louis Forain and two by Anders Zorn as well as others by lesser-known artists and people associated with Gregynog Press. It is not known how the sisters acquired these but they had a fashionable interest in print collecting and subscribed to the Print Collectors' Club. Gwendoline's trustees felt these works were not 'pictures' and were more suited to a library. Margaret and Gwendoline were themselves involved with fine book production at Gregynog Press and may have associated their prints with this area of their interests rather than their art collection. They were therefore given to the National Library of Wales, although Margaret was 'anxious that there should be an assurance from the Museum that they make no claim to them'.[36]

DISPLAY AND CONSERVATION

The sisters displayed their pictures as a joint collection, firstly at Plas Dinam, then at Gregynog and at their flat in London. At the time of Gwendoline's death many of the more valuable paintings were on loan to the National Library, but the majority of the works on paper were on display at Gregynog. Most of the watercolours and drawings, including those by Pissarro, Cézanne, Turner, Daumier, Maris, Gill, Blake, Clausen and Griffith were on display in the library there. After Gwendoline's paintings had been removed in 1952, the study and library remained popular places for the works on paper. *The Return of the Harvesters* by Lhermitte (*see Plate 3*) was hung in a prominent place in the entrance hall to the music room, but had moved to the study by the time of Margaret's death and was hung with a work of similar subject matter, Isräel's *Returning from the Fields*. They probably chose the library to display their watercolours and drawings due to the smaller size of the works, but it may also indicate that the sisters thought their drawings and watercolours necessitated close study.

Both of the sisters lent their works of art to various exhibitions and galleries, ranging from a loan of Cézanne paintings to the National Gallery of British Art to the loan of several Augustus John drawings to The Institute of Adult Education Exhibition at Coleg Harlech in 1935.[37] They were highly aware of the educational value of their collection and although it was a personal collection, it was never a private one. When the works were not on loan they were enjoyed by the constant visitors to Gregynog.

Robert Maynard managed the conservation of the works of paper in the collection. In 1949 he wrote to Gwendoline from London about work being undertaken on some of the drawings and etchings at the National Gallery. Although many of the works on paper were displayed, other works were obviously kept in a portfolio. Having seen a conservator of the National Gallery, he wrote, 'He tells me that the foxing (the reddish brown spots) cannot be entirely removed without damage to the paper but that he will do as much as he dare with safety… It is all over the mounts and the portfolio - I have asked him to supply new mounts, whilst he will treat the portfolio before returning the drawings.' He continued, 'The most difficult subject, he tells me, is the Innes water-colour which in its present state is ruined by the mass of spots in the sky'.[38]

CONCLUSIONS

The sisters do not seem to have acquired works on paper methodically, but collected them alongside their purchases of paintings and sculptures. Other collectors of the time, including Constantine Ionides, Hugh Lane and Samuel Courtauld, also acquired works on paper in this way. The sisters did not specialise in works from the Golden Age of Watercolour painting in Britain or in Old Master drawings. As with their oil paintings, they amassed works on paper by artists in the periods and styles in which they were interested, although many of the works are by artists who were distinguished in this field. Daumier, for example, worked as a caricaturist for many years, Augustus John was renowned for his drawings, Pissarro for his rapid figure studies and Lhermitte for his mastery of the medium of pastels.

Up until 1924 Gwendoline and Margaret had purchased watercolours and drawings in quantity to complement their oil painting collection: three Cézanne watercolours, four Daumier drawings, twelve Augustus John drawings. These were not necessarily systematic purchases, but choices made according to their own taste and preferences. Their purchases from this period almost fall into three categories: the watercolours which, as finished compositions, served the same purpose as the oil paintings (such as Signac, *St. Tropez*, Cézanne, *Bathers* (see *Plate 1*) and *The Diver* and the Turner landscapes); drawings by artists also represented by oil paintings in the collection, which are quite different from the paintings (such as the Pissarro figure studies and the Matthuis Maris pencil sketches); and works by artists renowned as draughtsmen (such as John and Daumier). The themes which recur throughout the watercolours and drawings collection echo the oil paintings - brightly coloured landscapes, such as Lhermitte, *The Return of the Harvesters* (see *Plate 3*), Signac, *St Tropez*; and figurative pictures, including the studies of Galway peasants by John, Daumier's *Head of a Man*, *A Lawyer, Walking*, and the Pissarro drawings. Peasants and people working the land appear both in landscapes and figure studies, for example, Isräels, *Returning from the Fields* and John, *Galway Peasants*.

Margaret's later, more systematic purchases tended to be single examples of particular artists' work. As a result Margaret's watercolours and drawings are much more varied, both in subject matter and style. Twenty-eight artists are represented in her bequest to the National Museum, compared with only five in Gwendoline's. New subject matters to the collection include *Female Nude* by Eric Gill (*see Plate 11*) and 18th-century topographical views by Moses Griffiths. The collection the sisters bestowed on the National Museum contains good examples by a variety of artists in different styles, different periods and from different countries. There are two main strengths to the collection, the 19th-century continental works and the modern works, particularly British, that Margaret added later.

The works on paper are only one part of Gwendoline's and Margaret's highly eclectic collecting. It incorporated paintings, modern ceramics, furniture, and Chinese, Egyptian and Persian pottery. Collecting itself was only one way in which the sisters expressed their overall interest in the arts and their desire to improve the standards of art in Wales. They wanted to offer the people of Wales a chance to learn and improve themselves. As Gwendoline said, 'We have so much to give that is not money'.[39] Their cultural projects include: opening their home, Gregynog, as a centre of artistic development; funding the Gregynog press to widen the knowledge of Welsh literature; inviting Belgian artist refugees to bring their talents to Wales (*see Plate 5*), and funding a number of initiatives at University College, Aberystwyth, including the Arts and Crafts department, the Arts and Crafts Museum and a music fellowship.

Gwendoline became somewhat frustrated with their efforts to improve artistic culture in Wales. She wrote, 'We have led the Welsh horse to the clearest brook we could possibly get, yet he has only tossed his head and walked straight through, stirring up all the mud and stones he could in doing so - he is so self-complacent, so self-sufficient - so ignorant - how are we ever to convince him that he is thirsty. That is the difficulty.'

Their watercolours and drawings form an integral part of the Davies collection. Both the first work of art[40] the sisters collected and the last[41] were watercolours. The collection was formed over a period of fifty-four years and it reflects the changes in interests and tastes of the sisters during this period. It is not known when the sisters decided to bequeath their art collection to the nation, but their first gift in 1940 is an early signifier. Urquhart also recalled Blaker's desire for the collection, 'I know he [Blaker] always hoped the pictures would go to Wales. He speaks of it in his private Diary'[42] The selections made by Gwendoline and Margaret Davies were personal ones but had a public purpose in mind, guided by various advisors and made possible by the dealers. As one critic of the time said, 'The Gregynog Collection bears testimony for that perfect dealer-advisor-collector relationship'.[43]

NOTES

1 *The Algerian* is now in the collection of the University of Wales.

2 Previous accounts of the Davies collection stated that it was begun in 1908.

3 He was created Baron Davies in 1932.

4 Calvinistic Methodists are a body of Christians of the Presbyterian order who claim to be the only denomination in Wales of a purely Welsh origin. The denomination's beginnings can be traced to the Rev. Griffith Jones (1684-1761) of Llanddowror, Carmarthenshire. Calvinists take a great interest in social, political and educational matters. Their chapels numbered 1641 in 1907.

5 Mark Evans, 'Gwendoline and Margaret Davies' for *Women in World History*, Yorkin Publications, [forthcoming].

6 Artist friend introduced to the sisters by Thomas Jones.

7 Consulting Curator of the Arts and Crafts Museum set up in 1918 and funded by the sisters as part of the Department of Arts and Crafts and the University College of Wales, Aberystwyth

8 NLW Gregynog collection vol 2, no 77.

9 Letter dated 6 April 1963, NMGW unpublished archive

10 Margaret's nickname was Daisy.

11 Undated letter from Hugh Blaker to Gwendoline Davies, NMGW unpublished archive.

12 Letter to Thomas Jones January 29 1925, NLW archive.

13 The Holburne of Menstrie Museum was housed at the Charlotte Street premises at this time. Although not well received by local press in Cardiff, the exhibition was well reviewed in the national papers and the attendance averaged over 500 visitors a day. Hugh Blaker wrote in his diary that the exhibition was 'a most stupendous show which should be a milestone in Welsh artistic development. About 50 pictures. The greatest thing of its kind seen in the Provinces.' (Murray Urquhart, 'The Blaker Diary: Some extracts with a memoir by Murray Urquhart' *Apollo,* 78 (1963), 293-8.)

14 John Witcombe taught at the School of Art in Bath and became a successful artist, working mostly in the medium of monotypes. He was a member of the Bath and West Country Society of Artists, frequently exhibiting with Hugh Blaker.

15 The choice of the Victoria Art Gallery, Bath can be explained by Blaker's friendship with Witcombe. He had left the Holburne Museum under unhappy circumstances, he had been unsuccessful in his application for the Keepership of Art at the National Museum of Wales and instead Isaac Williams was appointed, who was not an admirer of Impressionist paintings.

16 Letter from John Witcombe to Gwendoline, dated 24 April 1918, NMGW unpublished archive.

17 Entitled *Study of a Boy's Head* in the catalogue.

18 Blaker also acted on behalf of Gwendoline when she offered to lend some of her works to the National Gallery of British Art (now Tate Britain and Tate Modern). The Gallery at first refused the loan, a reflection of the attitude to Impressionism and Post-Impressionism in Britain at the time, which resulted in much debate and correspondence in the national newspapers and *The Burlington Magazine* between Hugh Blaker and the Gallery's Trustees. The paintings were eventually accepted on loan in 1922 and were the first works by Cézanne to be exhibited in a British National Gallery.

19 Blaker had a vivacious character and Urquhart sometimes felt he accepted all the credit for the development and care of the collection. According to Urquhart, Blaker '...was an egotist and was not happy to be out of the limelight'. He later recalled the 1913 exhibition at Cardiff and Bath, 'In his [Blaker's] remarks about the exhibition in 1912, he never speaks one word of the enormous part I took in bringing it about with the help of dear old Evan Hoyle' (Letter dated 14 September 1963, NMGW unpublished archive.)

20 The Gregynog Press was set up in 1921 by Gwendoline and Margaret to specialise in high quality, small editions of books. It hoped to produce examples of fine workmanship and develop interest in Welsh literature.

21 NMGW unpublished archive.

22 Emile Bernheim was the co-manager of Bernheim-Jeune, Paris.

23 John Ingamells, *The Davies Collection of French Art*, National Museum of Wales, Cardiff, 1967, p23.

24 NMGW unpublished archive.

25 Gwendoline did not make any distinctions between the oil paintings and the works on paper in her will. They were all termed 'pictures'.

26 Murray Urquhart, 'The Blaker Diary: Some extracts with a memoir by Murray Urquhart' *Apollo*, 78 (1963), 293-8.

27 Murray Urquhart, 'The Blaker Diary: Some extracts with a memoir by Murray Urquhart' *Apollo*, 78 (1963), 295.

28 Murray Urquhart, 'The Blaker Diary: Some extracts with a memoir by Murray Urquhart' *Apollo*, 78 (1963), 293-8.

29 NLW unpublished Gregynog archive collection.

30 Her will states:

'I GIVE AND BEQUEATH SUBJECT TO Estate and Legacy Duties (if any) payable theron on my death to the National Museum of Wales all the Pictures and Articles of Sculpture of National importance or Interest which shall be owned by me at the time of My death… If any question arises as to what are the Pictures and articles of Sculpture contained in this Bequest the decision of my Trustees theron shall be Final and Conclusive'

31 She attended the Slade School of Art and received private tuition at home. She would therefore have been more aware of artistic techniques.

32 CASW acquired twenty works whilst Margaret was acting as purchaser. She purchased works by the artists: John Elwyn, John Petts, Kyffin Williams, A. Beverley Burton, Ferdinand Cirel, Esther Grainger, Ray Howard Jones, Colin H.B. Jones, Will Roberts, Peter Coker, Leslie Moore, John Piper, Bromfield Rees and E. Morland Lewis.

33 Margaret's acquisition of this work is unknown.

34 Copy of letter dated February 1961 from Steegman to Margaret Davies, NMGW unpublished archive.

35 Margaret's will states:

'I GIVE AND BEQUEATH all my etchings prints and articles of sculpture (but excluding Jacob Epstein's Chia Pi (1942)) together with those paintings which I shall have specified in any Memorandum or Codicil… to the University of Wales for use at Gregynog hall… I GIVE AND BEQUEATH all my other paintings pictures and drawings of national importance… including the sculpture of Chia Pi… to the National Museum of Wales… I DECLARE that it is my desire that my paintings by modern artists shall be circulated and exhibited whenever and wherever possible '

36 NMGW unpublished archive.

37 The works lent were *Galway Peasants, Wayfarers, Studies of Children, Study of a Boy's Head.*

38 Letter dated 9 Dec 1949, NMGW unpublished archive. Both Innes watercolours now at the National Museum & Gallery show signs of foxing and mould treatment prior to arrival; this letter probably refers to *Canigou*.

39 Letter from Gwendoline Davies to Thomas Jones, 4th July 1923, NLW archive.

40 Hercules Brabazon Brabazon, *The Algerian* purchased in December 1906.

41 Oskar Kokoschka, *Landscape with Bonfire*, Robin Philipson, *The Rose Window* purchased in October 1962.

42 Letter dated 16 May 1963, NMGW unpublished archive.

43 Crieff Williamson, 'The Gwendoline E. Davies Bequest', *Art News and Review,* 5 (1953).

SELECTED BIBLIOGRAPHY

Anon, 'The Holburne Art Museum, Bath', *The Connoisseur*, 16 (1906), 263.

Hugh Blaker, 'The Drawings of Augustus John', *Colour*, 4 (1916), 122.

Peter Cannon-Brookes, 'The Davies Sisters of Gregynog', *Apollo,* 109 (1979), 221-6.

W.G. Constable, 'Modern Art at the Victoria Art Gallery, Bath', *The Burlington Magazine,* 36 (1920), 88-9.

Mark Evans, 'Gwendoline and Margaret Davies' for *Women in World History*, Connecticut.

Mark Evans, *Impressions of Venice from Turner to Monet*, National Museum of Wales, Cardiff and Lund Humphries, London, 1992.

Mark Evans, *Portraits by Augustus John, Family, Friends and the Famous*, National Museum of Wales, Cardiff, 1988.

Dorothy Harrop, *A History of the Gregynog Press*, Private Libraries Association, Cambridge, 1939.

John Ingamells, *The Davies Collection of French Art*, National Museum of Wales, Cardiff, 1967.

John Ingamells, 'The Margaret Davies Bequest to the National Museum of Wales', *The Connoisseur,* 156 (1964), 113-7.

Robert Meyrick, *Hugh Blaker*, Visual Art Department, University of Wales, Aberystwyth, 1991.

Susan Smithaman, *Belgian Artists in Wales 1914-1920*, unpublished B.A. dissertation, University of Wales, Aberystwyth, 1979.

John Stather, *Hugh Oswald Blaker: 1873-1936*, unpublished B.A. dissertation, University of Wales, Aberystwyth, 1990.

John Steegman, *Catalogue of the Gwendoline E. Davies Bequest*, National Museum of Wales, Cardiff, 1952.

John Steegman, 'The Gwendoline E. Davies Bequest', *The Connoisseur,* 129 (1952), 22-7.

Murray Urquhart, 'The Blaker Diary: Some Extracts with a Memoir by Murray Urquhart', *Apollo,* 78 (1963), 293-298.

M Vincentelli, 'The Davies Family and Belgian Refugee Artists & Musicians in Wales', *The National Library of Wales Journal*, 22 (1981), 226-233.

Eirene White, *The Ladies of Gregynog, Newtown, Powys*, University of Wales Press, Cardiff, 1985.

Plates

PLATE 1

Paul CÉZANNE (1839-1906)

Bathers

1875-7
watercolour, bodycolour and pencil on wove paper

The theme of the 'Bathers' recurred throughout Cézanne's career and works range in size from this small study to the *Grandes Baigneuses* in the National Gallery, London. It is a subject matter closely associated with Old Masters, and the monumental figures in this watercolour are much indebted to Rubens. Each figure has been worked out thoroughly in pencil and then coloured with watercolour and white highlights. It is a preliminary watercolour for a small oil painting now at the Musée d'Orsay. Cézanne wrote mounting instructions for this work below the image. The white highlights in this work have turned dark as a result of exposure to sulphur in the atmosphere possibly due to coal fires at Gregynog.

NMW A 1682

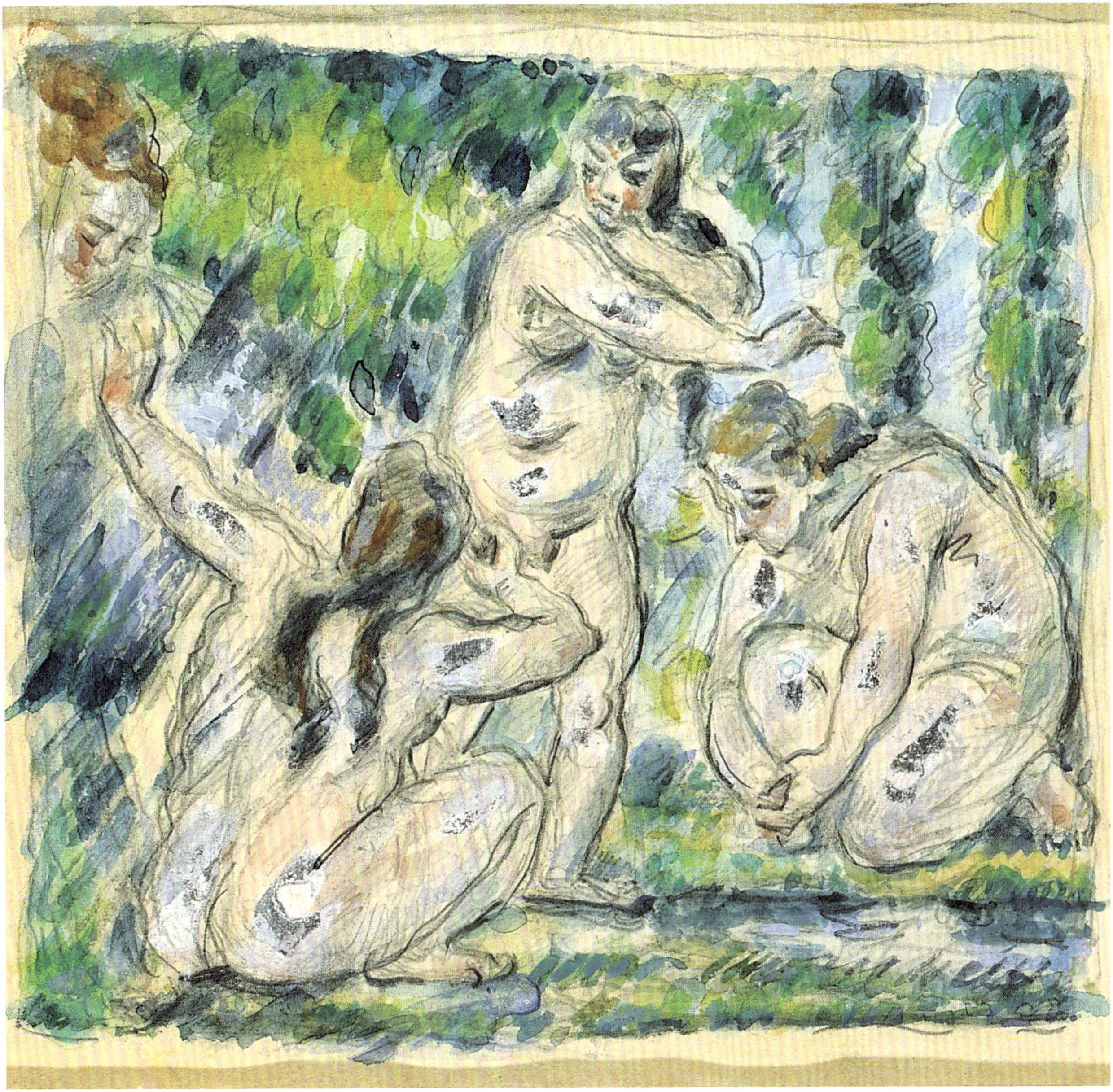

PLATE 2

Camille PISSARRO (1831-1903)

Two Studies of a Girl
c.1890
chalk on pink laid paper

Pissarro's graphic production increased enormously after 1880. He predominantly concentrated on the depiction of the human form and an increasing confidence is reflected in the greater variety of media in which he executed drawings after this date. In this study Pissarro has used different coloured chalks on pink paper to create a very strong, powerful image. The drawing shows the same model seen from the front and the back and as with most of his figure studies the composition relates directly to oil paintings: *Peasant Women Chatting in a Farmyard, Eragny* and *Peasant Women in a Farmyard.* Pissarro has carried out the modelling rapidly, but with great dexterity. He has concentrated on the poses of the figure rather than her character and thus only suggests her facial features.

This is one of six Pissarro drawings which Margaret Davies bought from a Leicester Galleries exhibition in June 1920. Two were bequeathed to the National Museum of Wales, the other four were sold at Sotheby's in 1960.

NMW A 1697

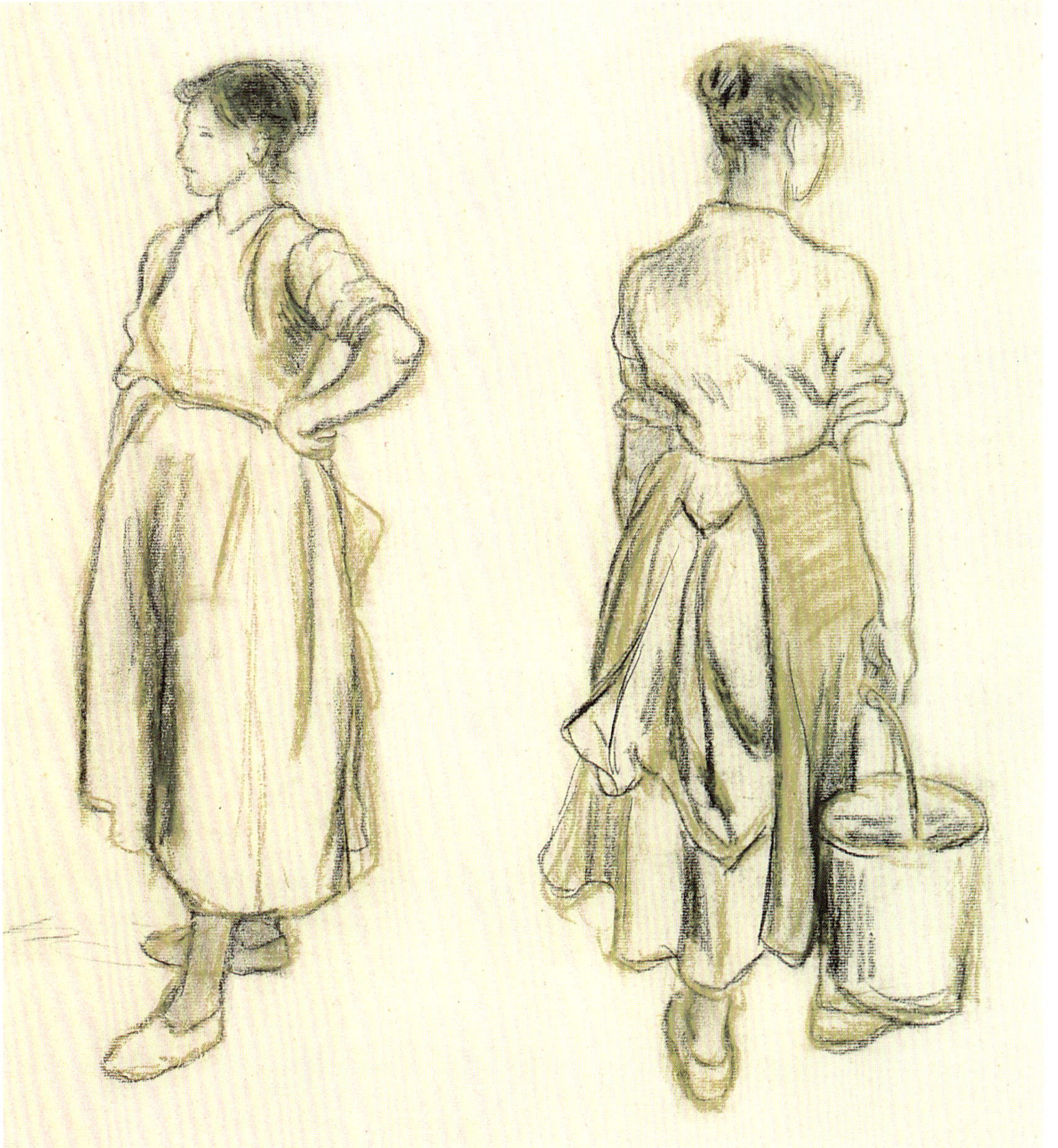

PLATE 3

Léon Augustin LHERMITTE (1844-1925)

The Return of the Harvesters
c.1911
pastel on paper on canvas

Lhermitte was a very prolific and successful artist, working and exhibiting both in France and Britain. He began to use pastels in the mid 1880s with great effect, helping to revolutionise the use of the medium. The generation of Degas rediscovered pastel and prized its spontaneity in capturing luminous effects. In this study Lhermitte has used pastel to capture the brilliant colours of the setting sun on the French landscape and the harvesters. The subject matter of rustic life is typical of his work and is much influenced by Jean-François Millet. Although a contemporary of many of the Impressionist artists he never exhibited at any of the Impressionist exhibitions. At the time of Margaret's death this work was hung in the study at Gregynog along with two other watercolours: Josef Israels, *Returning from the Fields* and Jan Hendrik van Mastenbrook, *Canal at Overschie, Setting Sun.*

NMW A 1692

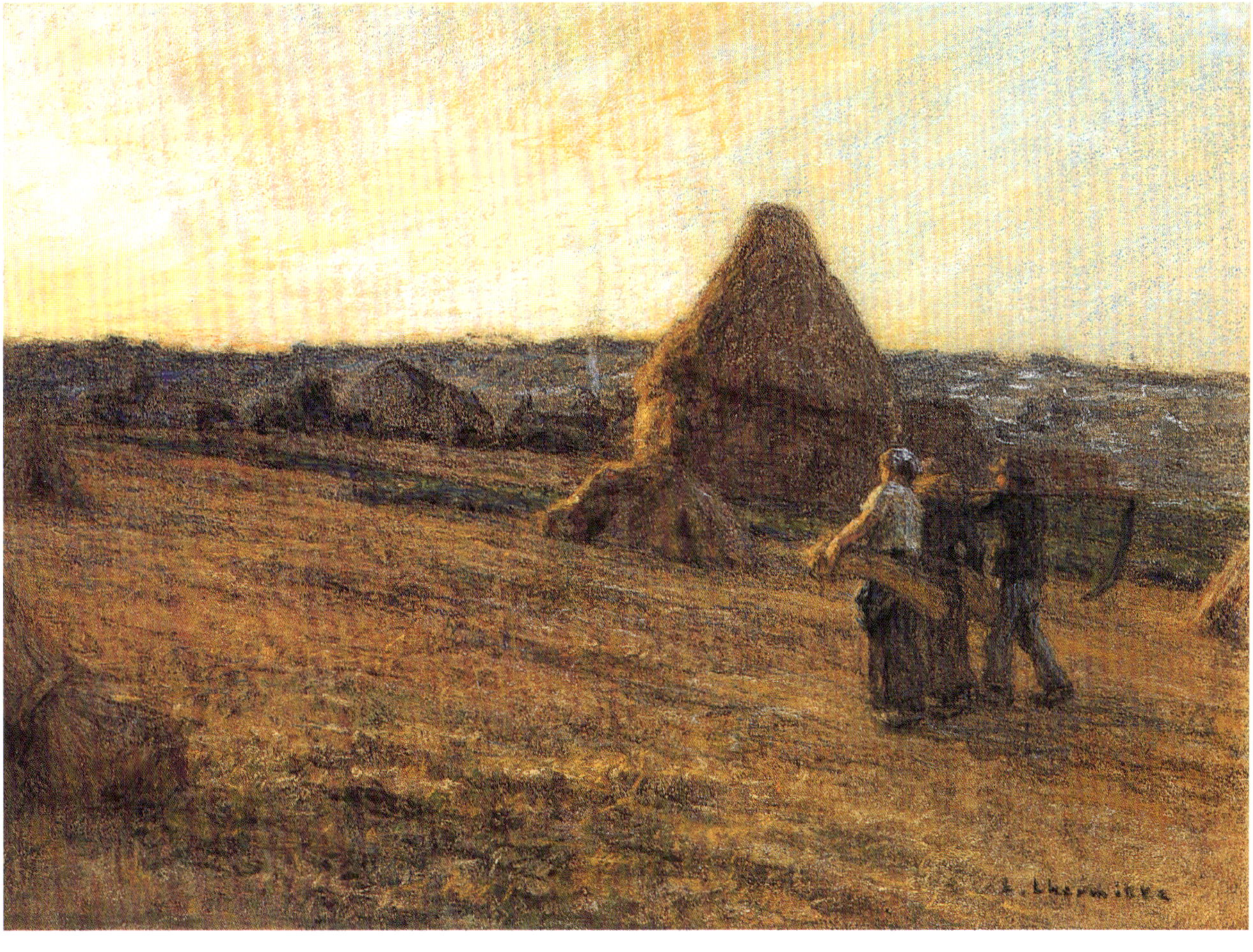
L. Lhermitte

PLATE 4

Honoré **DAUMIER (1808-1879)**

The Lawyer and his Client
c.1862-1864
crayon, pen and ink and watercolour on two sheets of laid paper joined together

Daumier almost exclusively depicted Parisian urban life and produced a series of works with legal subject matters. This work shows a woman anxiously consulting her lawyer in a corridor. Daumier's work as a caricaturist is particularly evident in the drawing of the two figures to the left, which were added after the two central figures. The expression of self-importance and satisfaction on the figure second from the left has been suggested with only a few lines.

In 1909 Hugh Blaker came back from Paris 'obsessed with Carrière, [and] Daumier'. Both of these artists are well represented in the Davies collection. Gwendoline bequeathed four works on paper by Daumier together with fourteen oil paintings.

NMW A 1679

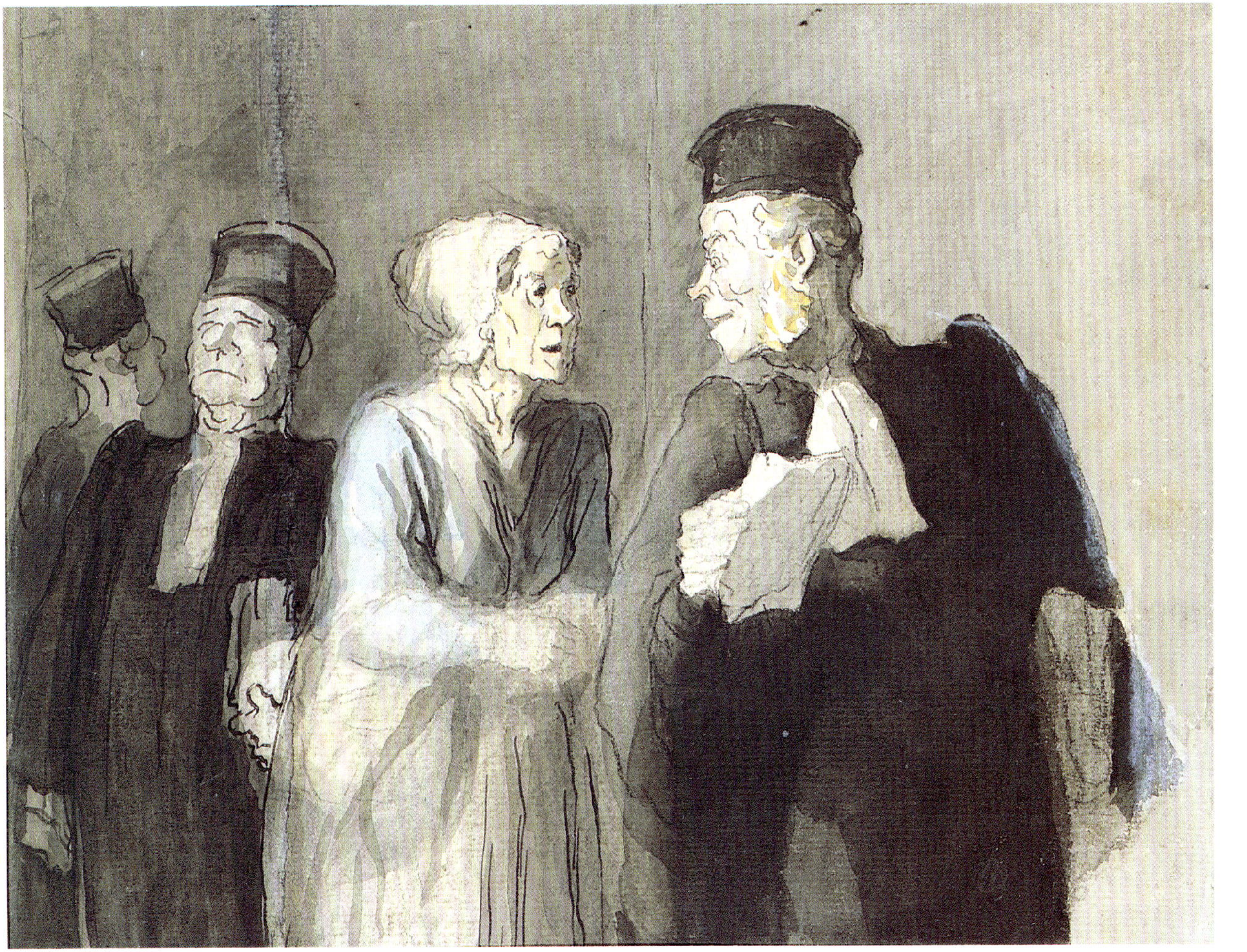

PLATE 5

Emile **FABRY (1865-1966)**

War
1914
crayon on wove paper

In February 1915 an exhibition of Belgian art formed part of the War Relief Exhibition at Burlington House, London. The exhibition was later brought to Cardiff. The Davies sisters probably purchased this work and another, Pierre Paulus, *The Flight*, from the Cardiff exhibition. This powerful, visionary image shows a dead soldier still holding a rifle being received into the arms of another figure. Belgium was overrun by Germany in August 1914 and artists there were immediately exposed to the horrors of the First World War.

NMW A 1689

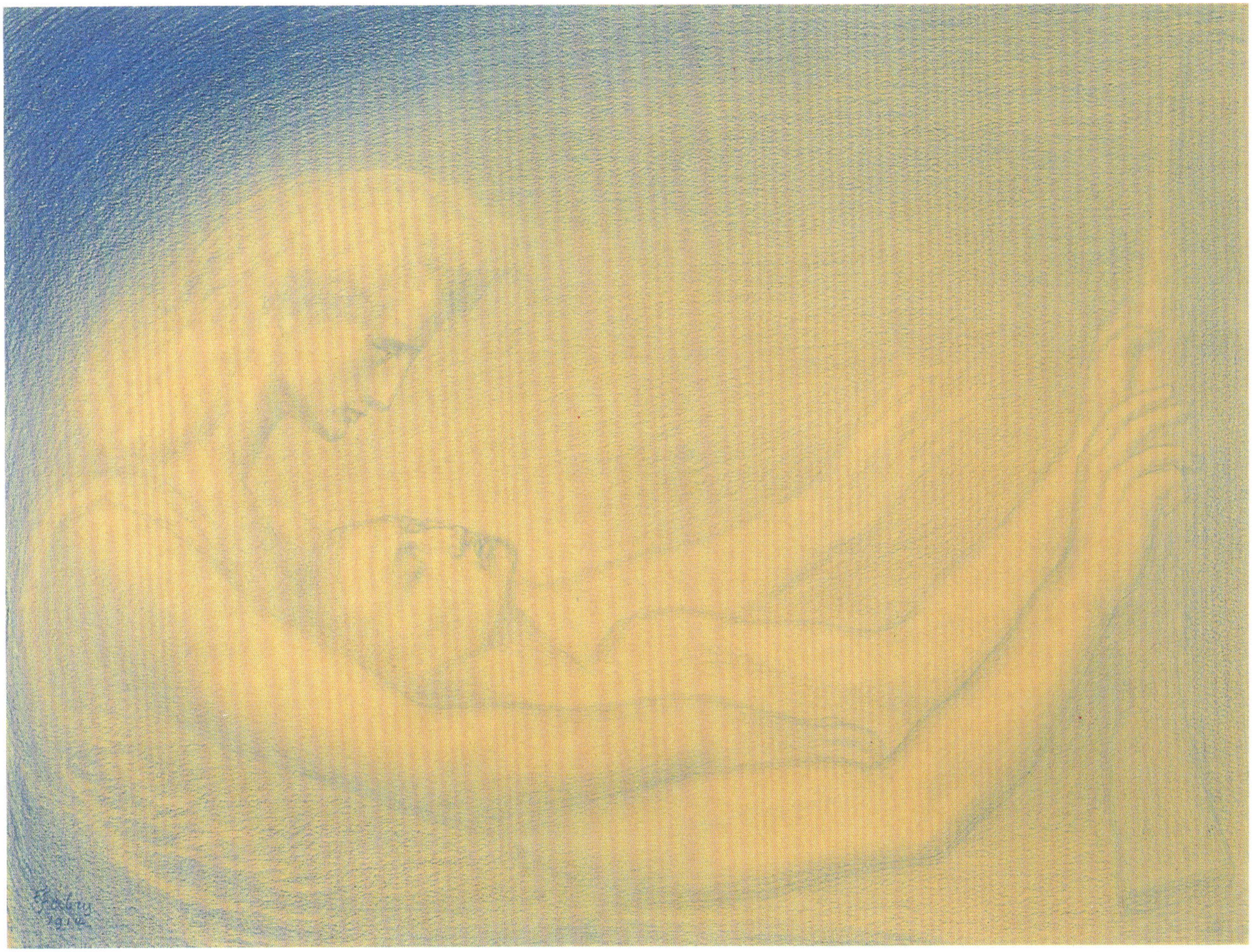

PLATE 6

William BLAKE (1757-1827)

Christ trampling down Satan

c.1800
ink and wash over pencil on wove paper

W.M. Rossetti listed this work in the first complete catalogue of Blake's work in 1863. The subject of the work has been disputed as *Christ trampling down Jehovah*, *Christ trampling down Urizen* and its present title. Blake trained for seven years as an engraver before entering the Royal Academy schools and this work is a drawing for an engraving, probably done by an assistant. The visionary quality of this fine drawing is characteristic of much of Blake's work. There are no records of the purchase of this work. It is the only work on paper of a religious subject that the sisters purchased.

NMW A 3992

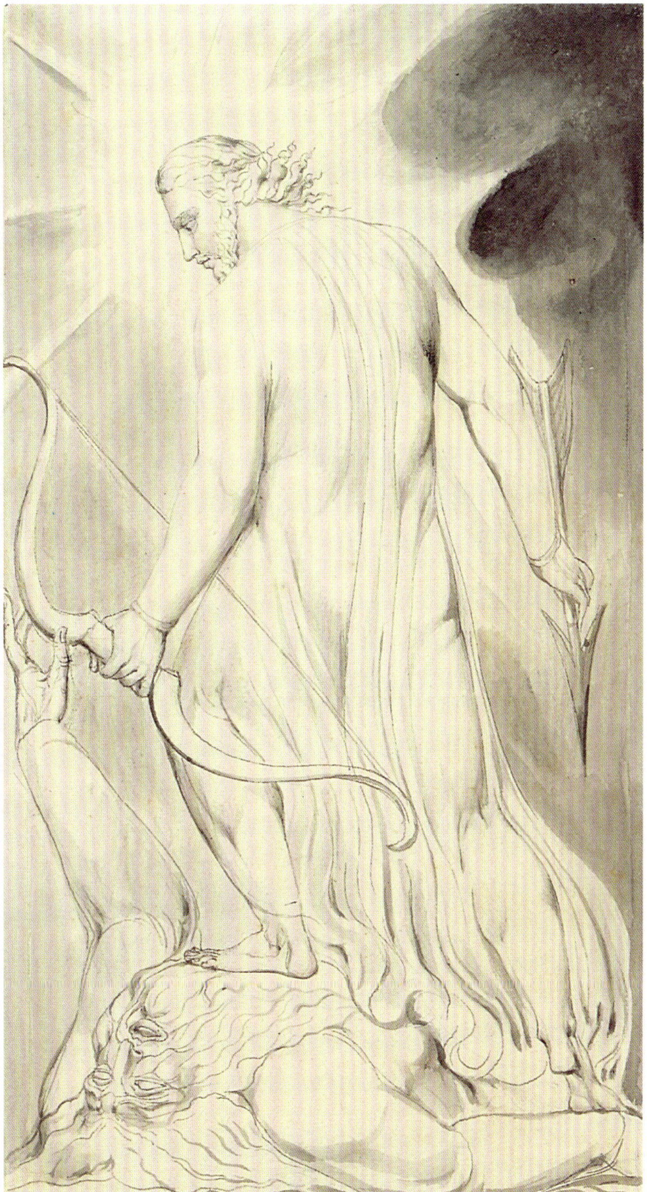

PLATE 7

Moses GRIFFITH (1747-1819)

Gregynog Hall
c.1789
watercolour and ink on wove paper with washline border

Moses Griffith was a self-taught artist employed by Thomas Pennant (1726-1798) from 1769 as a 'drawing man-servant'. Pennant was an antiquarian, historian and naturalist who published tours of Wales, Scotland and the Hebrides. Griffith accompanied him on all but one of these journeys recording the landscape, buildings and archaeological remains. This view shows the house built by the Blaney family in the 16th-century. By the time the sisters purchased Gregynog and its estate the house had been completely rebuilt. Only a fine panelled parlour from the original house was saved.

NMW A 3034

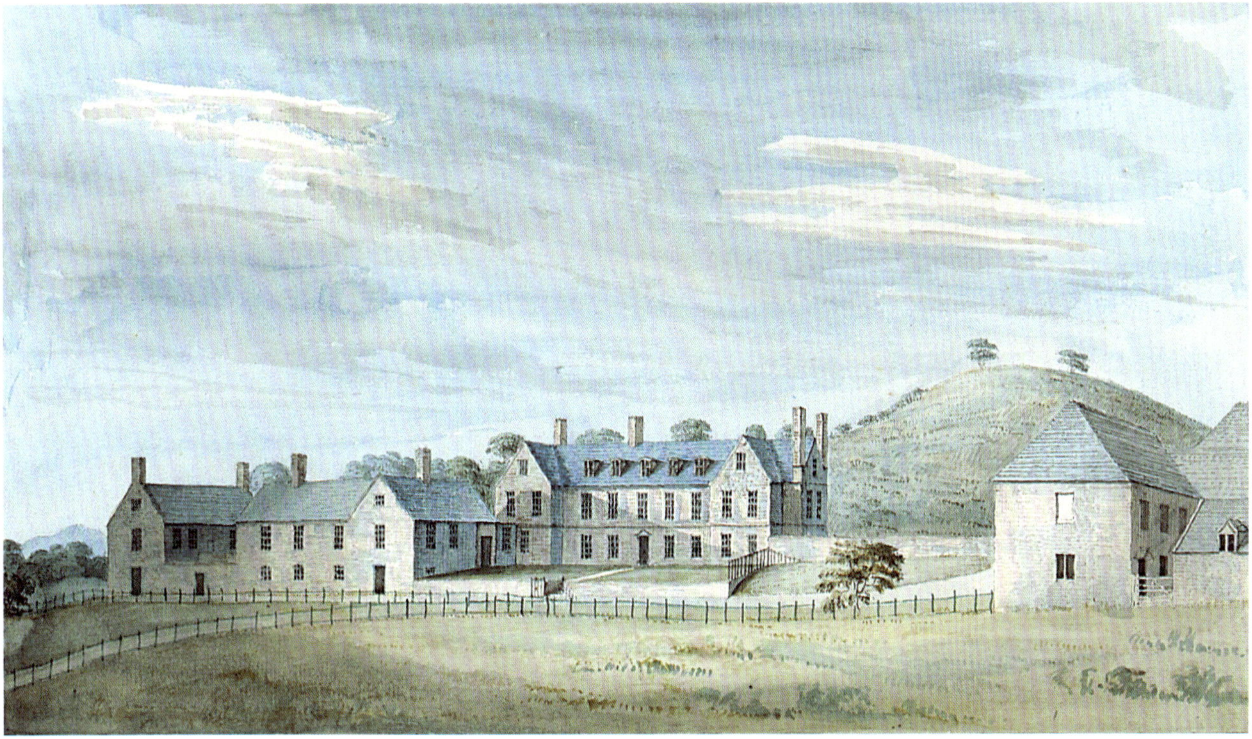

PLATE 8

Joseph Mallord William TURNER (1775-1851)

Rye, Sussex
1824
watercolour with scraping out on wove paper

This work exemplifies Turner's dramatic treatment of light and form. Rye, a picturesque town celebrated for its medieval buildings, is on the left, still in sunlight, whilst a storm coming in from the right causes the foreground to overshadow and people to hurry off the causeway to escape the rising waves. Men in the foreground, who were possibly mending the causeway, scramble to safety; one has fallen in the sea. This image was engraved by Edward Goodall for Turner's *Southern Coast*, 1824.

This is the first watercolour which Gwendoline purchased in 1908 and although they later acquired many 19th-century continental works, they continued to collect works by Turner until 1926.

NMW A 1742

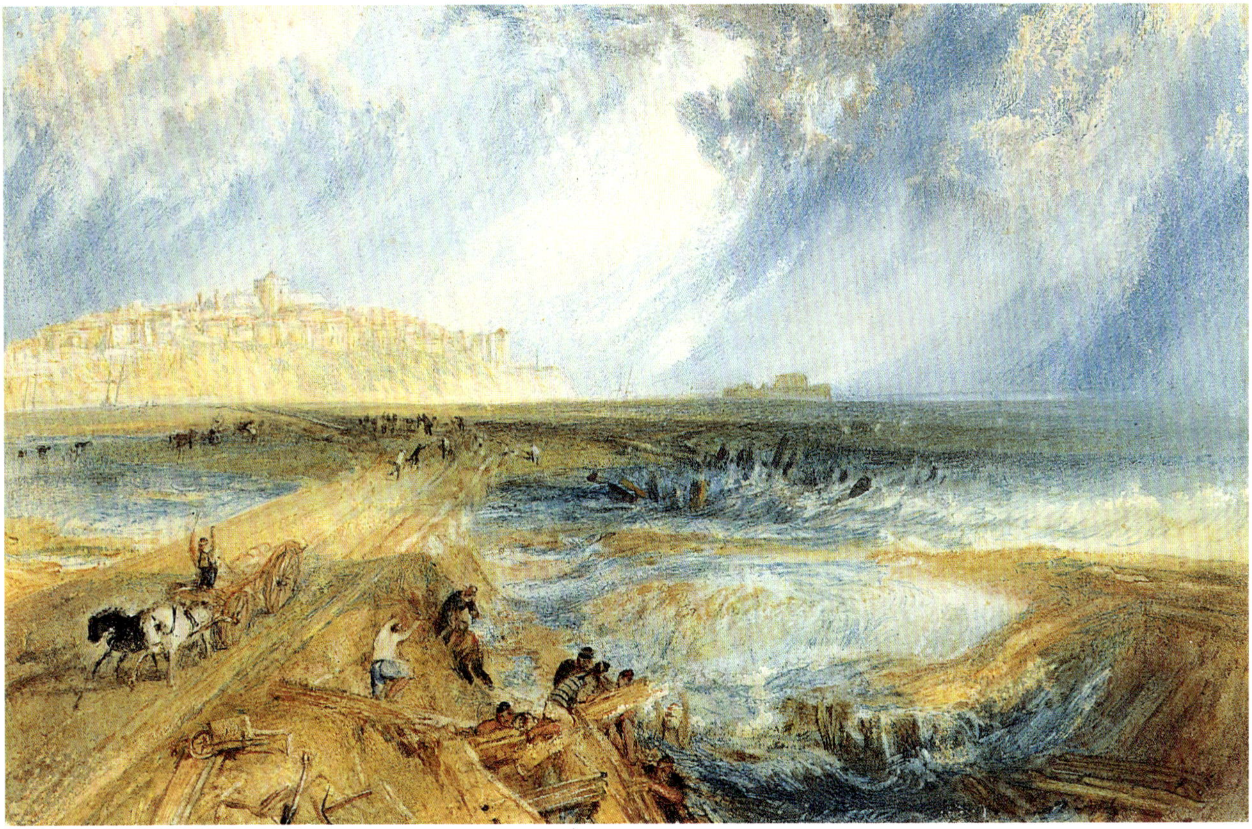

PLATE 9

Percy Wyndham LEWIS (1882-1957)

Ezra Pound
c.1921
pencil, watercolour and bodycolour on wove paper

Ezra Pound was an American poet and a literary scholar. He first met Wyndham Lewis in 1909. They shared many political and social views and propounded the principles of Modernism in art. Both were founding members of Vorticism, an English offshoot of Modernism, and together they published *Blast*, a magazine promoting the Vorticist manifesto. The sculptural shape of Pound's head, with his pointed beard, long nose and high forehead, lent itself to the geometric technique of Vorticism. The clarity of the outline has been accentuated by the use of graduated tones of wash to create form and volume. Lewis did numerous studies of Ezra Pound which culminated in an oil portrait in 1938, now in the Tate Gallery.

This is one of two portrait studies Margaret purchased from the Leicester Galleries in 1921. The other, *Study of a Woman*, remained at Gregynog and now belongs to the University of Wales.

NMW A 1867

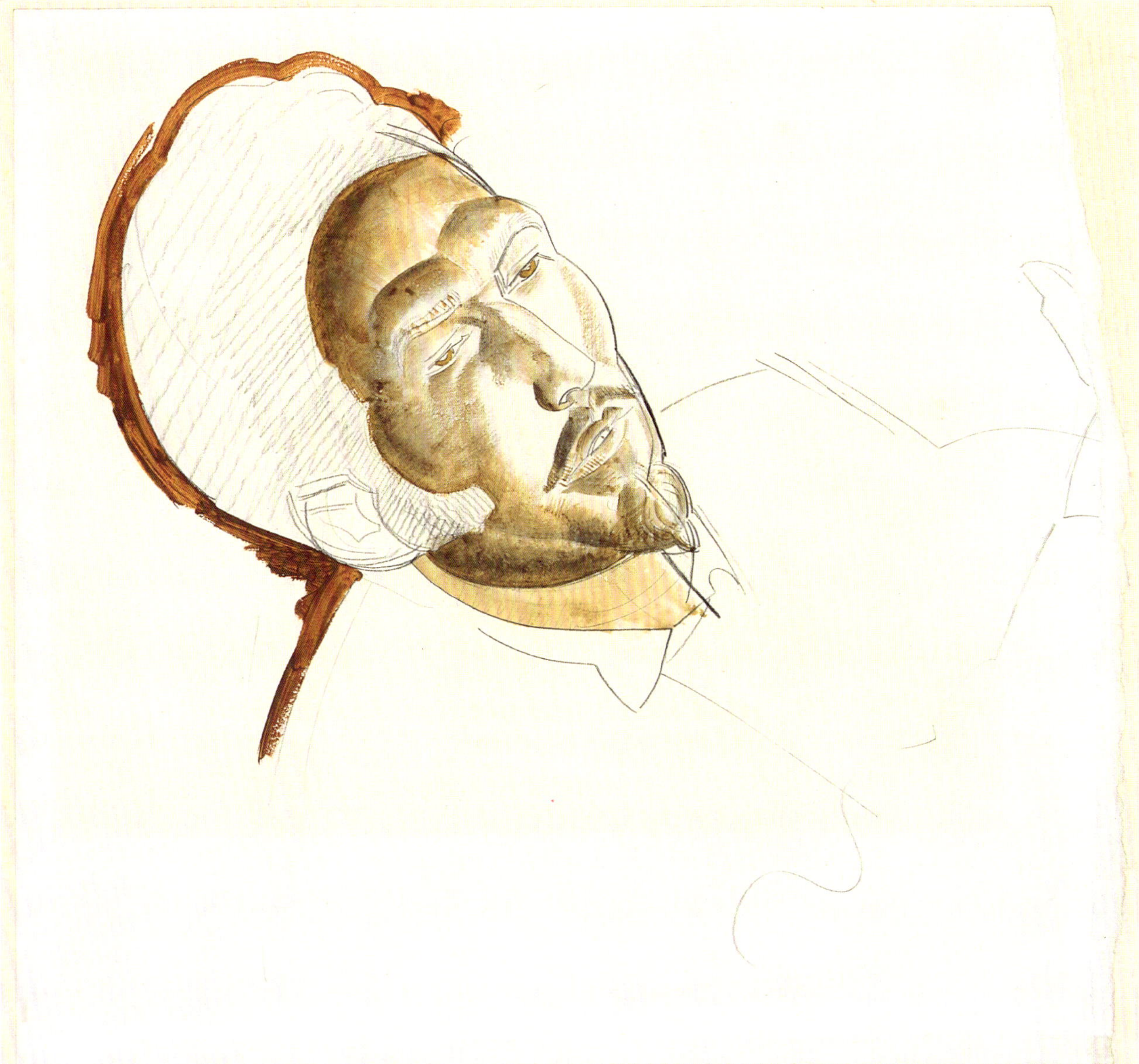

PLATE 10

HERMAN, Josef (1911-2000)

The Ox Cart
c.1950
ink and wash over pencil on laid paper

Born in Poland, Herman arrived in Glasgow as a refugee in 1940, unable to speak English. He came to Wales in 1944, settling in the village of Ystradgynlais. Although the mining community inspired Herman to produce some of his most celebrated work he was fascinated by the dignity of all aspects of physical labour. This bold, stark image of a monumental figure working the land is typical of his style. Interestingly, when selecting an example of his work for the collection in 1959, Margaret chose this rural scene and not an image of Welsh miners.

NMW A 14921

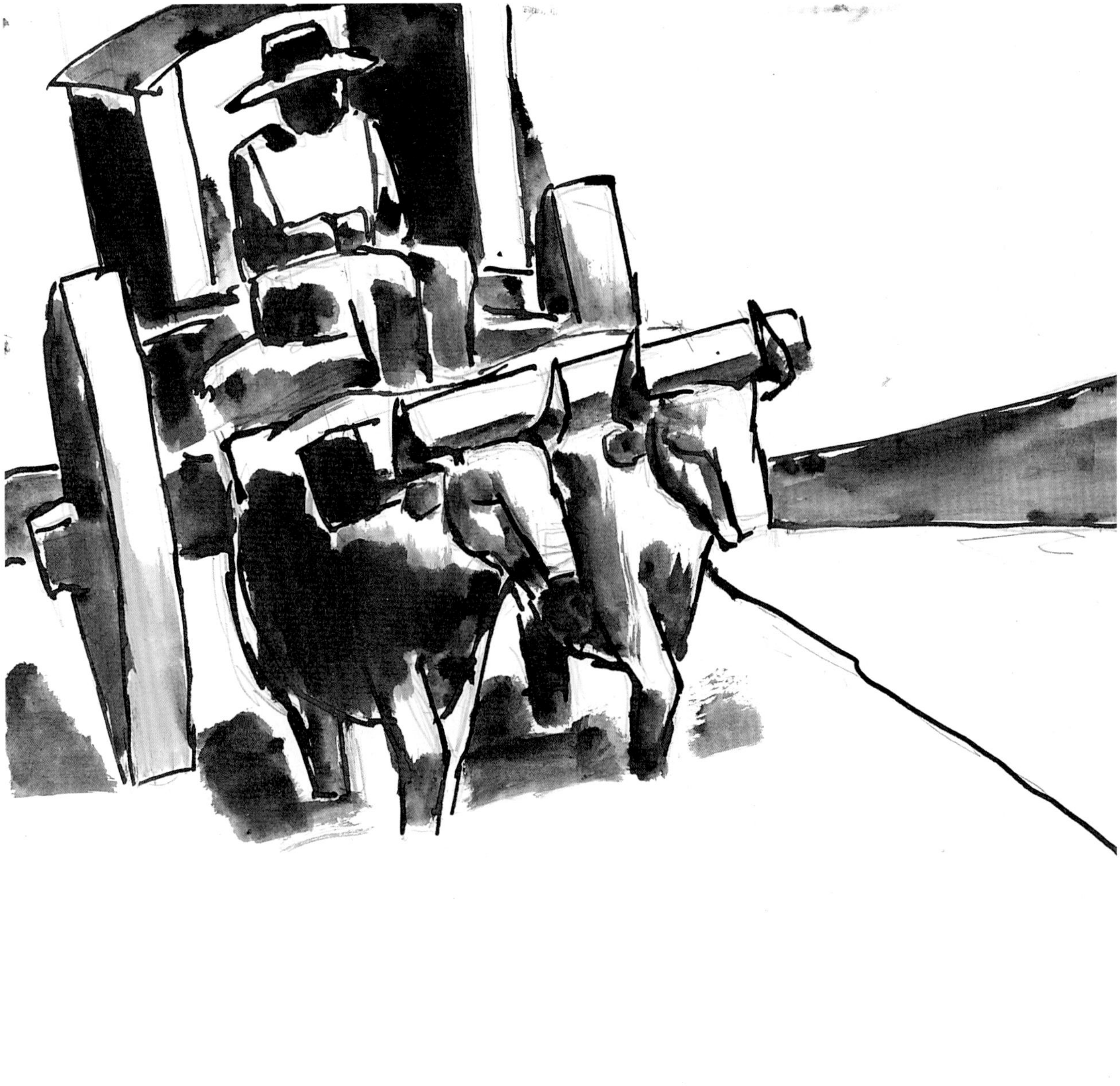

PLATE 11

Eric GILL (1882-1940)

Female Nude
1929
pencil on wove paper

In 1913 Eric Gill and his family moved to Ditchling Common where, with other artists and apprentices, they formed a Catholic guild of craftsmen dedicated to St Joseph and St Dominic. He later moved to Capel-y-ffin near Llantony, Monmouthshire setting up a similar settlement. Gill worked prolifically as a calligrapher, typographer, sculptor, wood-engraver and book designer. Later in his career, he produced a series of nude studies. He stated, 'drawing from life properly comes late in life rather than early for the training of imagination is the first thing to be seen to and this is best achieved by life and experience'. This work was hung in the annexe corridor of Gregynog, where the majority of the works on paper were displayed.

NMW A 5505

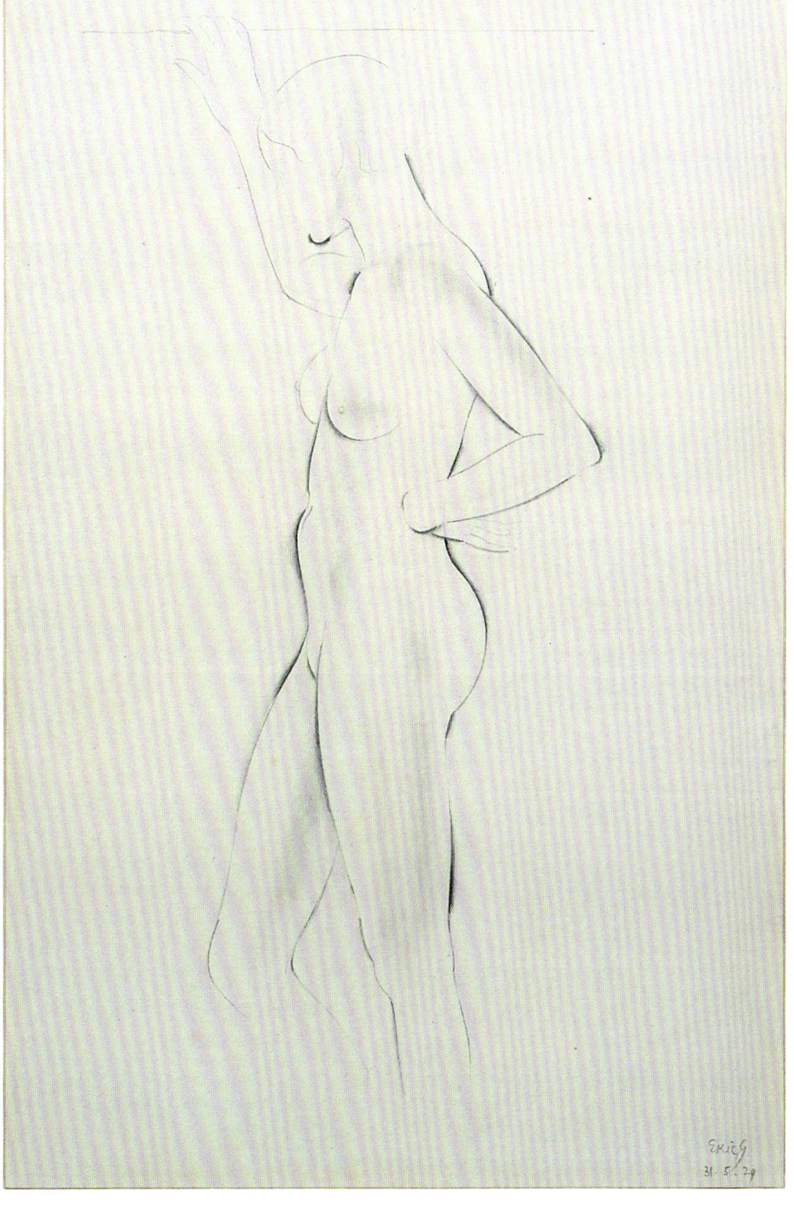
Eric G
31. 5. 29

PLATE 12

Augustus JOHN (1878-1961)

Dorelia McNeill as an Irish Girl
1915-16
pastel on wove paper

Unable to travel abroad during the First World War, John spent two months of 1915 in Galway. Here he conceived the idea of painting a vast picture about Galway and its people. The final work never materialised, but he executed numerous sketches and drawings. Some of these, including *Galway Peasants* and *Donegal Shawls*, entered the Davies collection. Though simply titled *An Irish Girl* when purchased by Margaret, the sitter in this drawing is certainly Dorelia McNeill (1881-1969). John experienced difficulty with the native models, which probably prompted Dorelia, his common-law wife, to model for him as an Irish girl with a Donegal shawl on his return. The peasant subject matter is one which recurs throughout the Davies collection. This work belonged to Hugh Blaker who had written an article about John's drawings for *Colour* in 1916.

Between them, Gwendoline and Margaret purchased 13 drawings by Augustus John. *Studies of a Child* was exhibited at the loan exhibition in Bath in 1918.

NMW A 1845

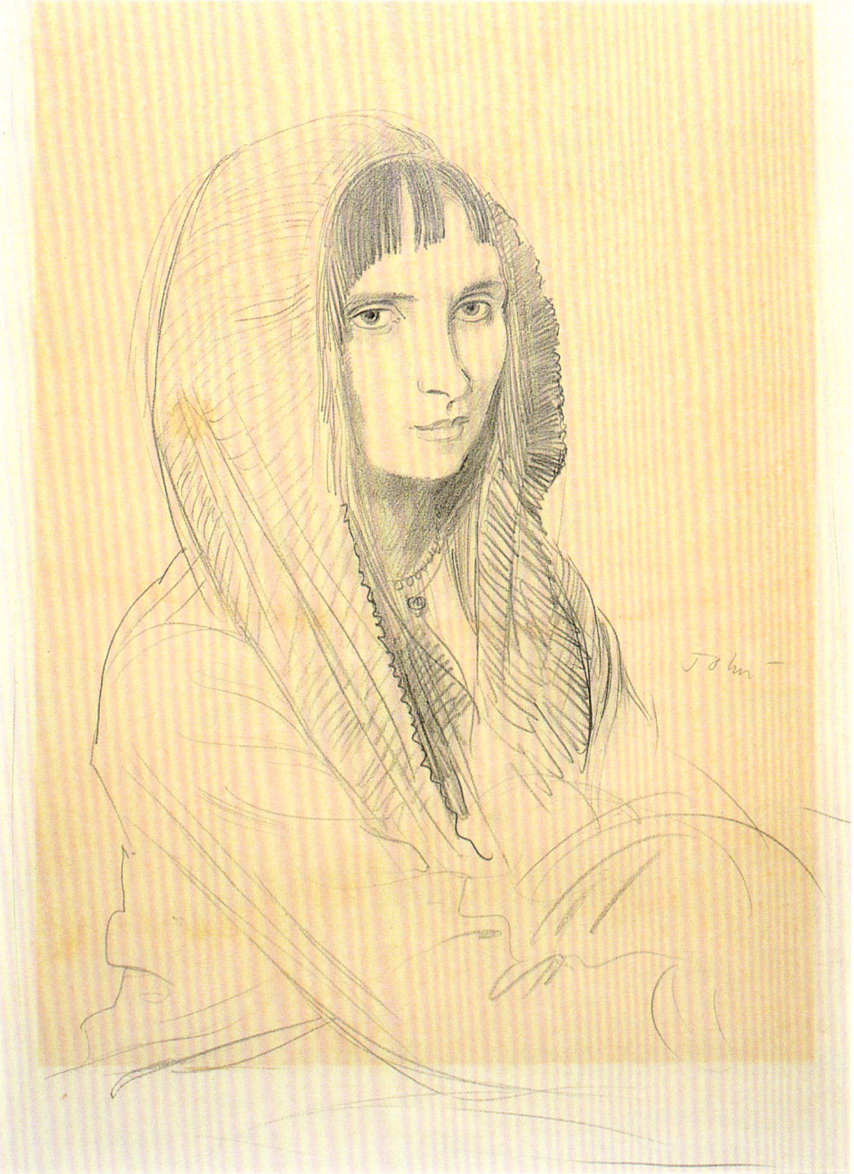
John

Catalogue

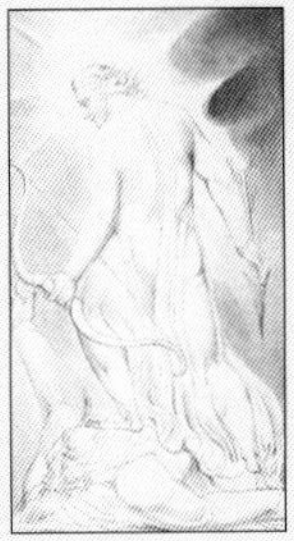

BLAKE, William
(1757-1827)

Christ Trampling Down Satan, c.1800

NMW A 3992
ink and wash over pencil on wove paper, 24.1 x 13.3
Bequeathed by Gwendoline Davies, 1952

Provenance: Mrs. Blake; ?Frederick Tathall; ?Joseph Hogarth; sold at Southgate's 7-30 June 1854, 10th evening, bought by H. Palser; ?Edward Chance by 1863; bought by Hugh Blaker for Gwendoline E. Davies.

Bibliography: William Michael Rossetti, 'Annotated Catalogue of Blake's Pictures and Drawings' in *Gilchrist, A Life of William Blake*, 2 vols, 1863 and 1880; NMW, *Catalogue of the Gwendoline E. Davies Bequest of Paintings, Drawings and Sculpture*, Cardiff, 1952, p.7, no.3; Martin Butlin, *The Paintings and Drawings of William Blake*, Yale University, 1981, p.372, no.526.

BOUDIN, Louis Eugène
(1824-1898)

Riverside Scene, Rotterdam

NMW A 1688
watercolour and pencil on laid paper, 16.8 x 20.9
signed
Bequeathed by Margaret Davies, 1963

Provenance: Lefevre & Son; sold to Margaret Davies 24 April 1924 at Exhibition no.104, for £7-0-0.

Bibliography: NMW, *Catalogue of the Margaret S. Davies Bequest of Paintings, Drawings and Sculpture*, Cardiff, 1963, p.38, no.109.

Previously titled *Old Houses at Honfleur*.

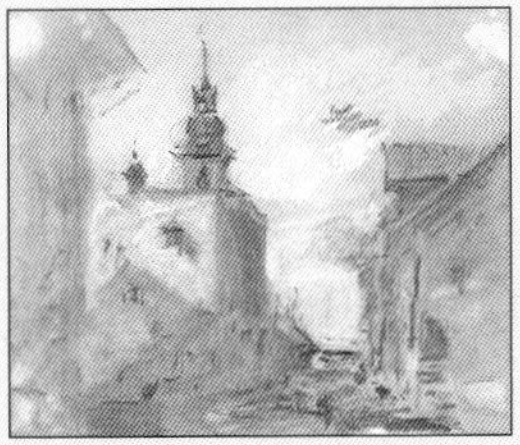

BRABAZON, Hercules Brabazon
(1821-1906)

Lucerne

NMW A 14925
pastel, chalk and pencil on wove paper, 18.5 x 22.4
signed
Bequeathed by Margaret Davies, 1963

Provenance: unknown, probably purchased by Gwendoline Davies between 1908 and 1927.

Bibliography: NMW, *Catalogue of the Gwendoline E. Davies Bequest of Paintings, Drawings and Sculpture*, Cardiff, 1952, p.38, no.110.

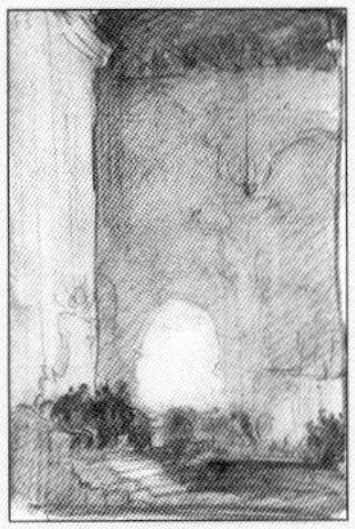

BRANGWYN, Sir Frank William
(1867-1956)

Interior of the Duomo, Taormina

NMW A 5605
watercolour, crayon and pencil on wove paper, 18 x 12.7
signed with initials
Bequeathed by Margaret Davies, 1963

Provenance: Fine Art Society, 1912; from whom purchased by Margaret Davies in November 1912 for £12.12.0.

Bibliography: NMW, *Catalogue of the Margaret S. Davies Bequest of Paintings, Drawings and Sculpture*, Cardiff, 1963, p.38, no.111.

Measurements are in centimetres. Bibliography is selected.

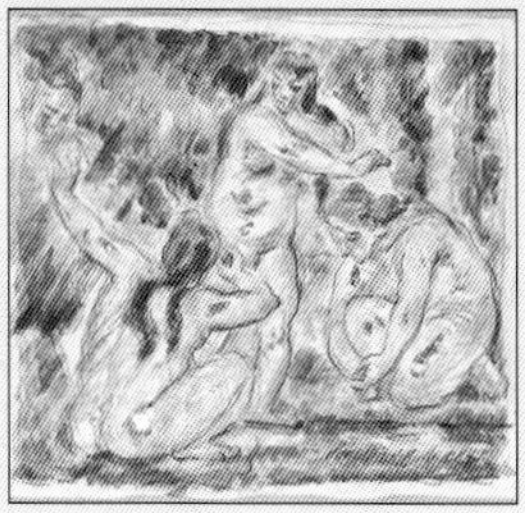

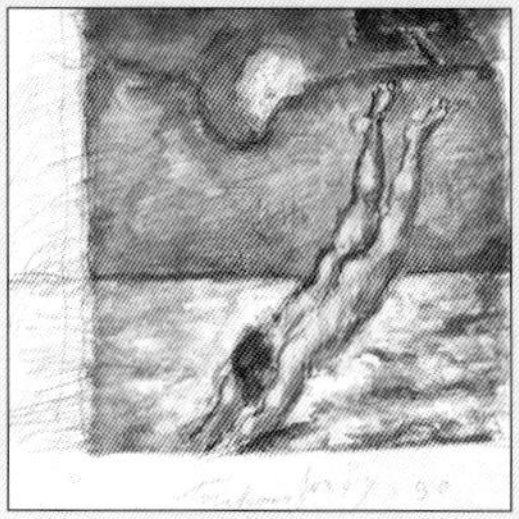

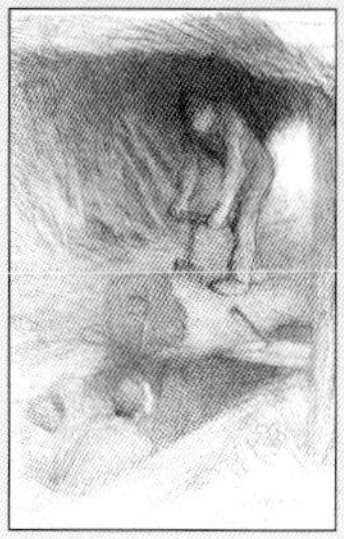

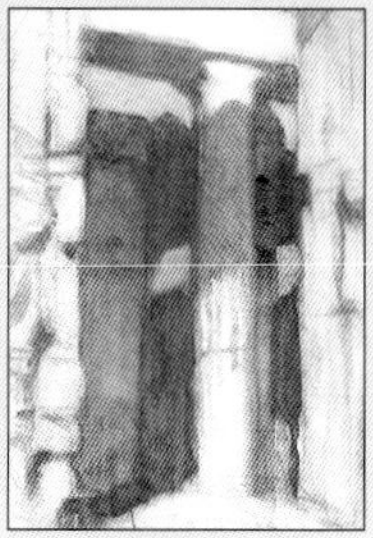

CÉZANNE, Paul
(1839-1906)

Bathers, 1875-7

NMW A 1682
watercolour, bodycolour and pencil on paper, 16.3 x 15.7
Bequeathed by Gwendoline Davies, 1952

Provenance: Ambroise Vollard; private collector, Paris; P. Hazard; 1-3 December 1919 sold at Galerie Georges Petit, no. 260 or 258 (?) to Galerie Bernheim-Jeune; from whom purchased by Gwendoline Davies for Fr 8,000, 12 March 1920.

Bibliography: NMW, *Catalogue of the Gwendoline E. Davies Bequest of Paintings, Drawings and Sculpture*, Cardiff, 1952, p.10, no.16; NMW, J. Ingamells, *The Davies Collection of French Art*, Cardiff, 1967, p.83-4, pl.34b; L.Venturi, *Cézanne. Son art - son oeuvre*, San Francisco, 1989, pl.239, no. 818; M.L Krumrine, *Paul Cézanne, The Bathers*, Basel/Eidolon, 1989, p.137, no.76, (illus) no.102.

CÉZANNE, Paul
(1839-1906)

The Diver, 1867-70

NMW A 1683
watercolour, bodycolour over pencil on wove paper, 15.6 x 16.2
verso: sketch of two men in pencil
Bequeathed by Gwendoline Davies, 1952

Provenance: P. Hazard; 1-3 December 1919 sold at Galerie Georges Petit, no. 257 to Galerie Bernheim-Jeune; from whom purchased by Gwendoline Davies for Fr 8,000, 12 March 1920.

Bibliography: NMW, *Catalogue of the Gwendoline E. Davies Bequest of Paintings, Drawings and Sculpture*, Cardiff, 1952, p.10, no.17; NMW, J. Ingamells, *The Davies Collection of French Art*, Cardiff, 1967, p.83, pl.34a; L.Venturi, *Cezanne. Son art - son oeuvre*, San Francisco, 1989, p.239, no.818.

Previously titled *La Chute d'Icare.*

CLAUSEN, George
(1852-1944)

The Saw Pit

NMW A 14924
pencil and crayon with scratching out on wove paper, 41.8 x 27.6
signed
Bequeathed by Margaret Davies, 1963

Provenance: The French Gallery; from whom purchased by Margaret Davies, June 1912.

Bibliography: NMW, *Catalogue of the Margaret S. Davies Bequest of Paintings, Drawings and Sculpture*, Cardiff, 1963, p.39, no.113.

CLAUSEN, George
(1852-1944)

West Door of the Parthenon by Moonlight

NMW A 14923
charcoal and watercolour on wove paper, 25.5 x 17.8
signed
Bequeathed by Margaret Davies, 1963

Provenance: Royal Society of Water Colour Painters, November, 1912 (225); from where purchased by Margaret Davies.

Bibliography: NMW, *Catalogue of the Margaret S. Davies Bequest of Paintings, Drawings and Sculpture*, Cardiff, p.38, no.112.

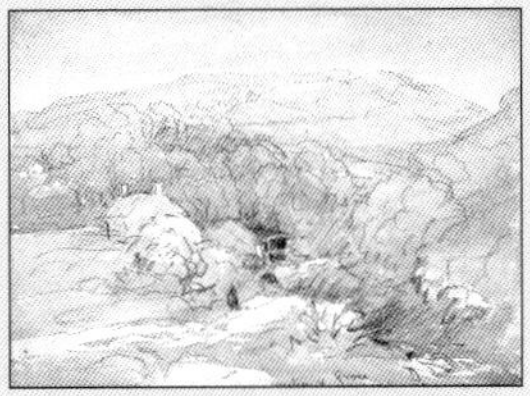

COX, David
(1783-1859)

Melin y Groes near Conway

NMW A 14922
pencil and wash on wove paper, 20.5 x 28
Bequeathed by Margaret Davies, 1963

Provenance: Agnew's 1954; purchased by Margaret Davies in December, 1954 for £10.10.0

Bibliography: NMW, *Catalogue of the Margaret S. Davies Bequest of Paintings, Drawings and Sculpture*, Cardiff, 1963, p.39, no.114.

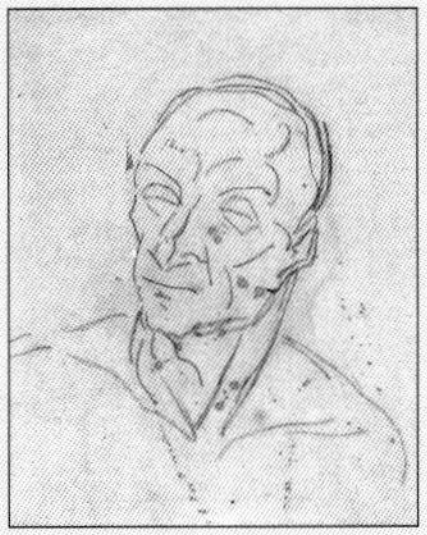

DAUMIER, Honoré
(1808-1879)

Head of a Man

NMW A 1680
black chalk on laid paper, spotted with iron gall ink, 18.5 x 15.0
Bequeathed by Gwendoline Davies, 1952

Provenence: Lemaire; unknown Paris dealer; Lefevre & Son; from whom purchased by Gwendoline Davies with 2 other Daumier drawings (NMWA 1678 & 1681) for £200, 16 December1922.

Bibliography: NMW, *Catalogue of the Gwendoline E. Davies Bequest of Paintings, Drawings and Sculpture*, Cardiff, 1952, p.13, no.36(a); K.E. Maison, *Honoré Daumier, Catalogue Raisonné of the Paintings, Watercolours and Drawings*, Thames & Hudson, London, 1968, vol.II, p.32, no.30.

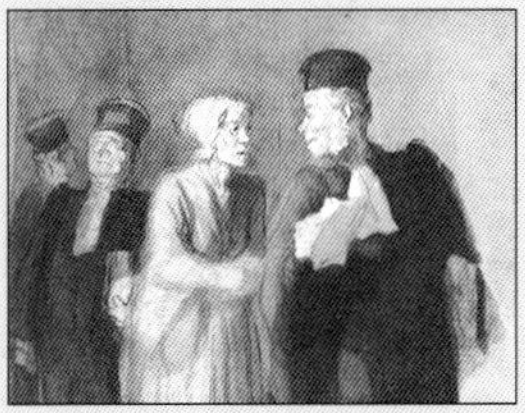

DAUMIER, Honoré
(1808-1879)

The Lawyer and his Client

NMW A 1679
watercolour, ink and crayon on laid paper, 24.1 x 23.8
Bequeathed by Gwendoline Davies, 1952

Provenance: Jules Castagnary, Paris; Durand-Ruel, Paris; Paul Rosenberg, Paris; sold to Bernheim-Jeune, Paris, 3 April 1918; from whom purchased for £450 by Gwendoline Davies, 8 March 1920

Bibliography: NMW, *Catalogue of the Gwendoline E. Davies Bequest of Paintings, Drawings and Sculpture*, Cardiff, 1952, p.13, no.34; K.E. Maison, Honoré Daumier, *Catalogue Raisonné of the Paintings, Watercolours and Drawings*, Thames & Hudson, London, 1968, vol.II, p.205, no.617, pl.233; National Gallery of Canada, *Daumier*, 1999, p.366-367, no.216.

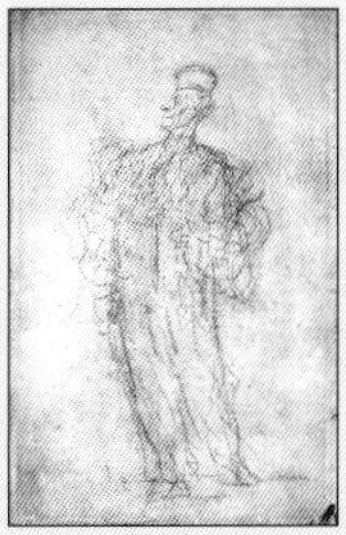

DAUMIER, Honoré
(1808-1879)

A Lawyer, walking

NMW A 1681
ink and chalk on laid paper, 40 x 26.3
Bequeathed by Gwendoline Davies, 1952

Provenance: Lemaire; unknown Paris Dealer; Lefevre & Son; from whom bought by Gwendoline Davies with 2 other Daumier drawings (NMWA 1678 & 1680) for £200, 16 December1922

Bibliography: NMW, *Catalogue of the Gwendoline E. Davies Bequest of Paintings, Drawings and Sculpture*, Cardiff, 1952, no.35; K.E. Maison, *Honoré Daumier, Catalogue Raisonné of the Paintings, Watercolours and Drawings*, Thames & Hudson, London, 1968, vol.II, p.190, no.570.

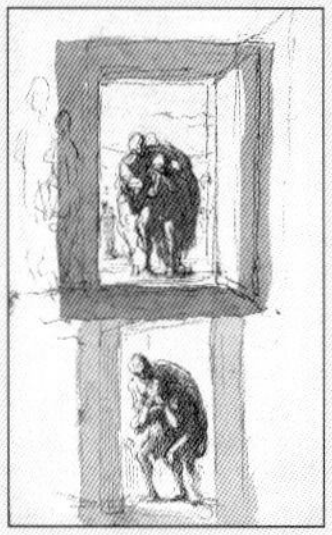

DAUMIER, Honoré
(1808-1879)

Two studies for the Return of the Prodigal Son, 1863

NMW A 1678
ink and wash on laid paper, 20.9 x 13.1
Bequeathed by Gwendoline Davies, 1952
verso: two sketches of the head of an old man.

Provenance: Lemaire; unknown Paris dealer; Lefevre & Son; from whom bought by Gwendoline Davies 16 December 1922.

Bibliography: NMW, *Catalogue of the Gwendoline E. Davies Bequest of Paintings, Drawings and Sculpture*, Cardiff, 1952, p.13, no.36(b); K.E. Maison, *Honoré Daumier, Catalogue Raisonné of the Paintings, Watercolours and Drawings*, Thames & Hudson, London, 1968 vol.II, no.756; National Gallery of Canada, *Daumier*, 1999, p.339, no.191.

Previously titled *The Good Samaritan* and *The Blind Man and the Cripple*.

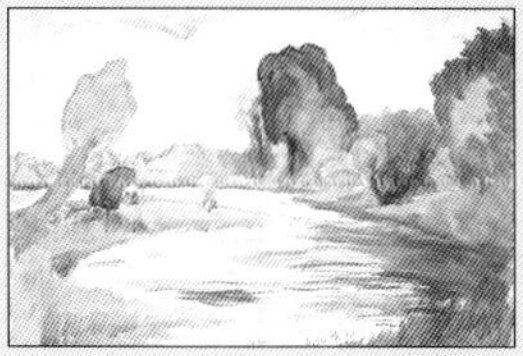

DUNLOP, Ronald Ossary
(1894-1973)

The Arun, 1961

NMW A 14583
watercolour on wove paper, 37.5 x 56.0
signed and dated
Bequeathed by Margaret Davies, 1963

Provenance: unknown; in Davies Collection by 1963.

Bibliography: NMW, *Catalogue of the Margaret S. Davies Bequest of Paintings, Drawings and Sculpture*, Cardiff, 1963, p.39, no.115.

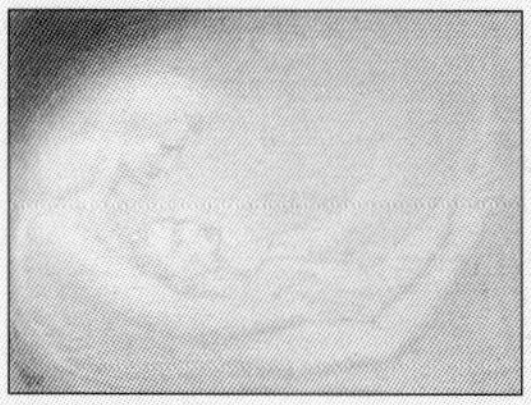

FABRY, Emile
(1865-1966)

War, 1914

NMW A 1689
crayon on wove paper, 28.2 x 38
signed and dated
Bequeathed by Margaret Davies, 1963

Provenance: unknown, probably purchased from the exhibition of Belgian art, Cardiff, 1915.

Bibliography: NMW, Catalogue of an exhibition of Belgian art, Cardiff, 1915, no.80(?);: NMW, *Catalogue of the Margaret S. Davies Bequest of Paintings, Drawings and Sculpture*, Cardiff, 1963, p.39, no.116; M.Vincenteli, 'The Davies family and Belgian refugee artists and musicians in Wales', *The National Library of Wales Journal*, 22 (1981-82), 226-233.

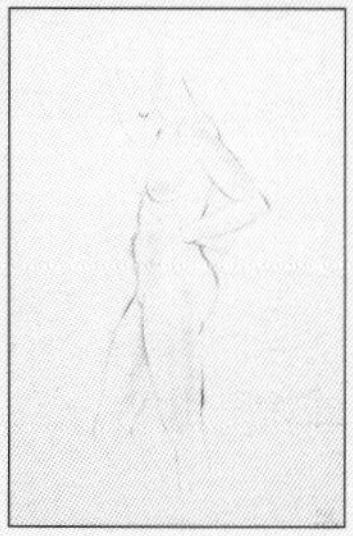

GILL, Eric
(1882-1940)

Female Nude, 1929

NMW A 5505
pencil on wove paper, 45.8 x 30.6
signed and dated
Bequeathed by Margaret Davies, 1963

Provenance: The Goupil Gallery, 1929; purchased by Margaret Davies for £10.10.0, work titled *Nude*, ex. no 49.

Bibliography: NMW, *Catalogue of the Margaret S. Davies Bequest of Paintings, Drawings and Sculpture*, Cardiff, 1963, p.40, no. 117.

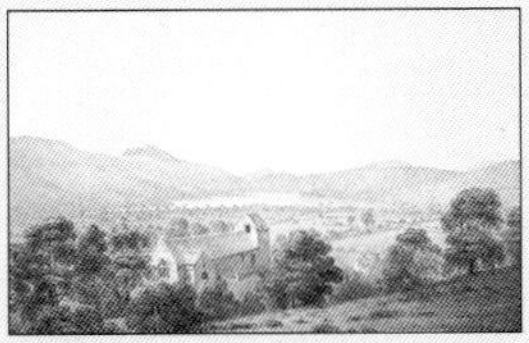

GRIFFITH, Moses
(1747-1819)

Bala Pool, 1805

NMW A 14706
watercolour over pencil on wove paper with black wash border, 24 x 37.9
verso: sketches of Cader Idris, Arran Penllyn, Arran Morddu, Arennig, Mynydd Nodd
Bequeathed by Margaret Davies, 1963

Provenance: Thomas Pennant; David Pennant; by descent to Viscount Feilding; Christie's 1938; from where purchased by Walker Galleries Ltd.; from whom purchased by Margaret Davies, February 1939.

Bibliography: NMW, *Catalogue of the Margaret S. Davies bequest of Paintings, Drawings and Sculpture*, NMW, Cardiff, 1963, p.41, no 124; Welsh Arts Council, *Moses Griffith: Artist and Illustrator in the Service of Thomas Pennant*, 1979, no.1.

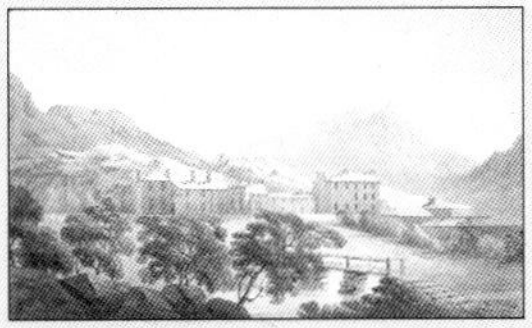

GRIFFITH, Moses
(1747-1819)

Capel Curig, Caernarvon, 1806

NMW A 3193
watercolour over pencil on wove paper, 27.5 x 46.5
signed and dated
Bequeathed by Margaret Davies, 1963

Provenance: Thomas Pennant; David Pennant; by descent to Viscount Feilding; Christie's 1938; from where purchased by Walker Galleries Ltd.; purchased by Margaret Davies, February 1939.

Bibliography: NMW, *Catalogue of the Margaret S. Davies Bequest of Paintings, Drawings and Sculpture*, Cardiff, 1963, p.41, no.122; Welsh Arts Council, *Moses Griffith: Artist and Illustrator in the Service of Thomas Pennant*, 1979, no.9.

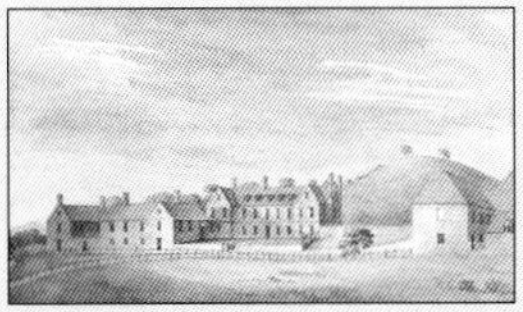

GRIFFITH, Moses
(1747-1819)

Gregynog Hall, c.1789

NMW A 3034
watercolour and ink on wove paper with washline border, 24.7 x 41
signed
Bequeathed by Margaret Davies, 1963

Provenance: Thomas Pennant; David Pennant; by descent to Viscount Feilding; Christie's 1938; from where purchased by Walker Galleries Ltd; purchased by Margaret Davies, February 1939.

Bibliography: NMW, *Catalogue of the Margaret S. Davies Bequest of Paintings, Drawings and Sculpture*, Cardiff, 1963, p.40, no.121.

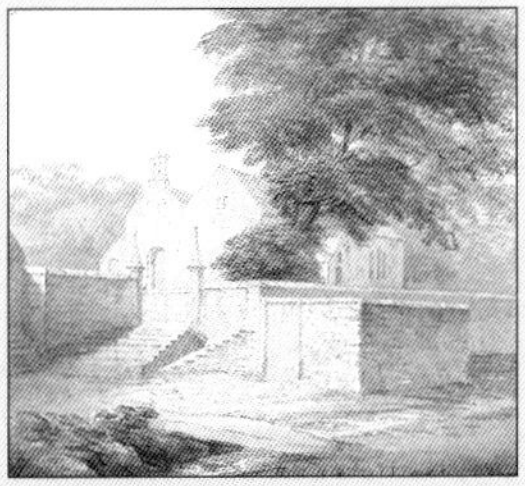

GRIFFITH, Moses
(1747-1819)

Llan St Fraid, Denbighshire

NMW A 14586
watercolour over pencil on wove paper, 27.8 x 30.7
signed
Bequeathed by Margaret Davies, 1963

Provenance: Thomas Pennant; David Pennant; by descent to Viscount Feilding; Christie's 1938; from where purchased by Walker Galleries Ltd.; purchased by Margaret Davies, February 1939.

Bibliography: NMW, *Catalogue of the Margaret S. Davies Bequest of Paintings, Drawings and Sculpture*, Cardiff, 1963, p.40, no.118; Welsh Arts Council, *Moses Griffith: Artist and Illustrator in the Service of Thomas Pennant*, 1979, no.29.

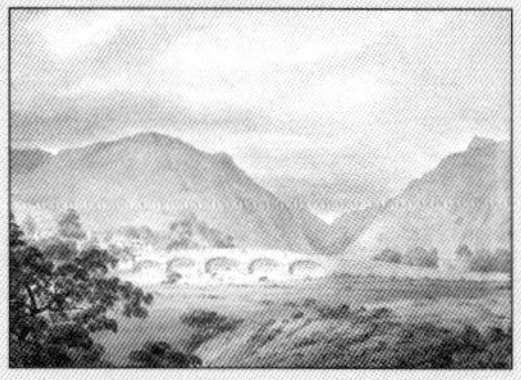

GRIFFITH, Moses
(1747-1819)

Llanelltyd Bridge, Merionethshire

NMW A 14937
watercolour over pencil on wove paper, 25.5 x 37
Bequeathed by Margaret Davies, 1963

Provenance: Thomas Pennant; David Pennant; by descent to Viscount Feilding; Christie's 1938; from where purchased by Walker Galleries Ltd.; purchased by Margaret Davies, February 1939.

Bibliography: NMW, *Catalogue of the Margaret S. Davies Bequest of Paintings, Drawings and Sculpture*, Cardiff, 1963, p.41, no.124; Welsh Arts Council, *Moses Griffith: Artist and Illustrator in the Service of Thomas Pennant*, 1979, no.27.

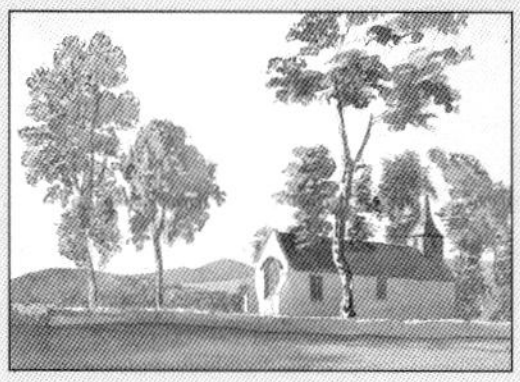

GRIFFITH, Moses
(1747-1819)

Nannerch Church

NMW A 3149
watercolour over pencil on laid paper with black wash border, 26.1 x 36.2
Bequeathed by Margaret Davies, 1963

Provenance: Thomas Pennant; David Pennant; by descent to Viscount Feilding; Christie's 1938; from where purchased by Walker Galleries Ltd.; purchased by Margaret Davies, February 1939.

Bibliography: NMW, *Catalogue of the Margaret S. Davies Bequest of Paintings, Drawings and Sculpture*, Cardiff, 1963, p.40, no.119.

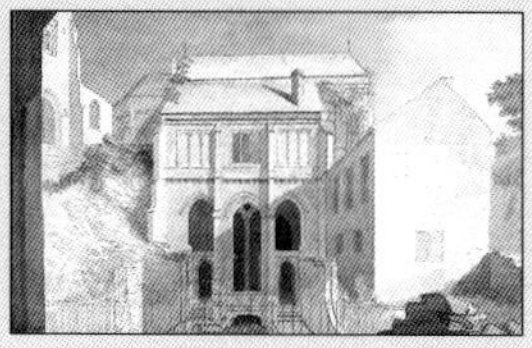

GRIFFITH, Moses
(1747-1819)

St. Winifred's Well, Holywell

NMW A 3370
watercolour and ink over pencil on laid paper, surrounded by wash line border, 29.6 x 44.6
Bequeathed by Margaret Davies, 1963

Provenance: Thomas Pennant; David Pennant; by descent to Viscount Feilding; Christie's 1938; from where purchased by Walker Galleries Ltd.; purchased by Margaret Davies, February 1939.

Bibliography: NMW, *Catalogue of the Margaret S. Davies Bequest of Paintings, Drawings and Sculpture*, Cardiff, 1963, p.40, no.120; Welsh Arts Council, *Moses Griffith: Artist and Illustrator in the Service of Thomas Pennant*, 1979, no.24.

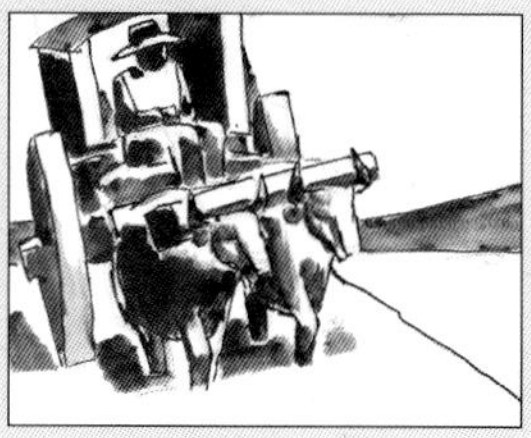

HERMAN, Josef
(1911-2000)

The Ox Cart

NMW A 14921
ink and wash over pencil on laid paper, 20.4 x 25.3
Bequeathed by Margaret Davies, 1963

Provenance: Roland, Browse and Delbanco, November, 1959; from whom bought by Margaret Davies for £26.5.0

Bibliography: NMW, *Catalogue of the Margaret S. Davies Bequest of Paintings, Drawings and Sculpture*, Cardiff, 1963, p.41, no.125.

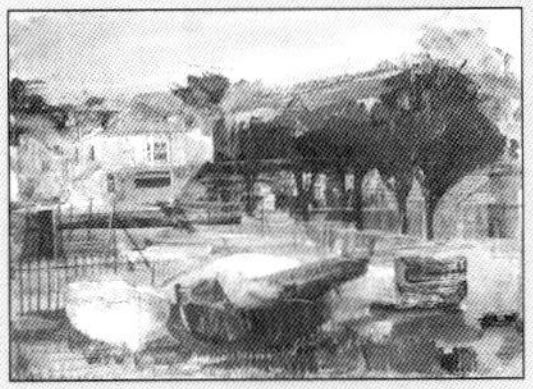

HOWARD JONES, Ray
(1903-1996)

The Antelope, Mumbles, 1959

NMW A 14438
watercolour, bodycolour, chalk and pencil on wove paper, 38.5 x 54.4
signed and dated
Bequeathed by Margaret Davies, 1963

Provenance: South Wales Group, January 1961; from where purchased by Margaret Davies for £17.17.0.

Bibliography: NMW, *Catalogue of the Margaret S. Davies Bequest of Paintings, Drawings and Sculpture*, Cardiff, 1963, p.42, no.103.

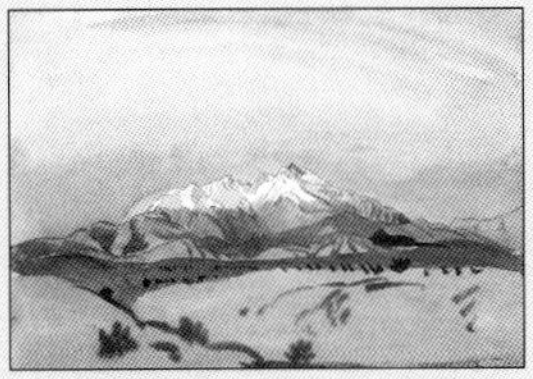

INNES, James Dixon
(1887-1914)

Canigou, 1912

NMW A 14919
ink and watercolour on paper, 25.4 x 35.4
signed and dated
Bequeathed by Margaret Davies, 1963

Provenance: Redfern Gallery; from where purchased by Margaret Davies, November 1939.

Bibliography: NMW, *Catalogue of the Margaret S. Davies Bequest of Paintings, Drawings and Sculpture*, Cardiff, 1963, p.41, no.126.

Previously titled *Welsh Mountains*.

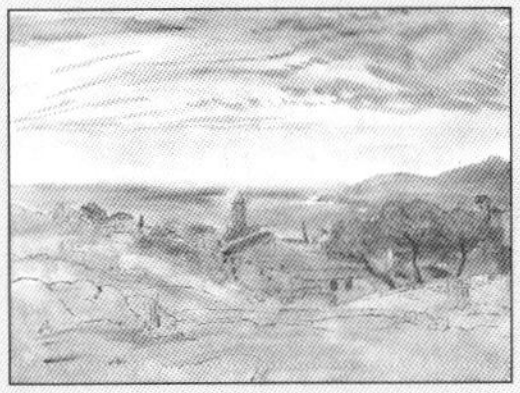

INNES, James Dixon
(1887-1914)

Collioure

NMW A 14705
watercolour and ink on wove paper, 27.9 x 38.8
Bequeathed by Margaret Davies, 1963

Provenance: The Leicester Galleries; from where purchased by Margaret Davies, February, 1952 (3).

Bibliography: NMW, *Catalogue of the Margaret S. Davies Bequest of Paintings, Drawings and Sculpture*, Cardiff, 1963, p.41, no.127.

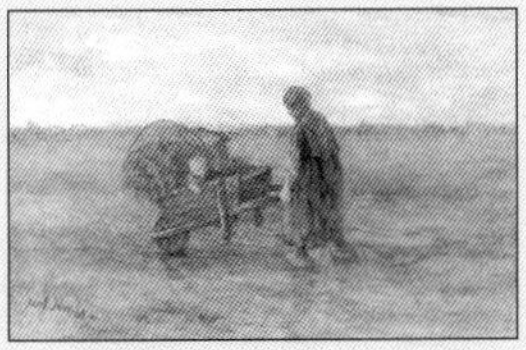

ISRÄELS, Joseph
(1824-1911)

Returning from the Fields

NMW A 1690
watercolour and bodycolour on wove paper, 21.5 x 34
signed
Bequeathed by Margaret Davies, 1963

Provenance: Alexander Young; sold at Christies, 30 June 1910 (lot 12) to Hugh Blaker acting on behalf of Margaret Davies.

Bibliography: NMW, *Catalogue of the Margaret S. Davies Bequest of Paintings, Drawings and Sculpture*, Cardiff, 1963, p.92, no.128.

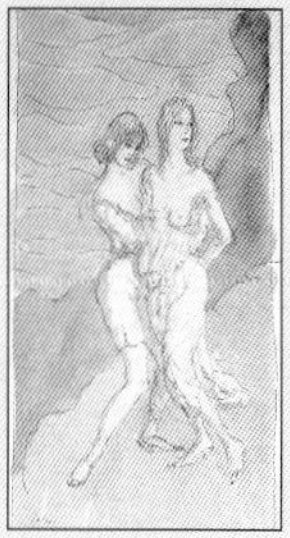

JOHN, Augustus
(1878-1961)

Amantes Délaissées

NMW A 14931
watercolour and ink on wove paper, 50.9 x 35.5
signed
Bequeathed by Gwendoline Davies, 1952

Provenance: Chenil Galleries; from where purchased by Gwendoline Davies, December 1919.

Bibliography: NMW, *Catalogue of the Gwendoline E. Davies Bequest of Paintings, Drawings and Sculpture*, Cardiff, 1952, p.17, no.55.

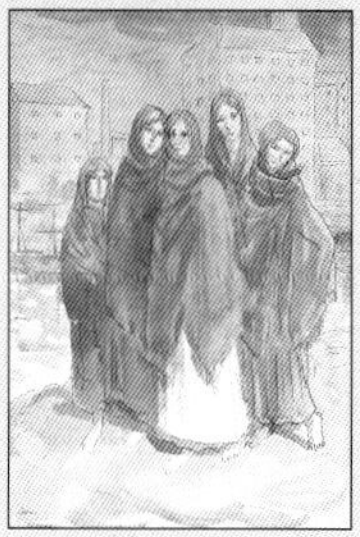

JOHN, Augustus
(1878-1961)

Donegal Shawls

NMW A 3663
watercolour and ink (faded) on wove paper, 45.6 x 31.6
signed
Bequeathed by Gwendoline Davies, 1952

Provenance: Coll. T. Sands Johnson; sold at Christie's 19 May 1926 (41); ?Messrs Sampson; ?Hugh Blaker; Gwendoline Davies.

Bibliography: NMW, *Catalogue of the Gwendoline E. Davies Bequest of Paintings, Drawings and Sculpture*, Cardiff, 1952, p.17, no.59; NMW, *Themes and Variations: the drawings of Augustus John*, Cardiff, 1996.

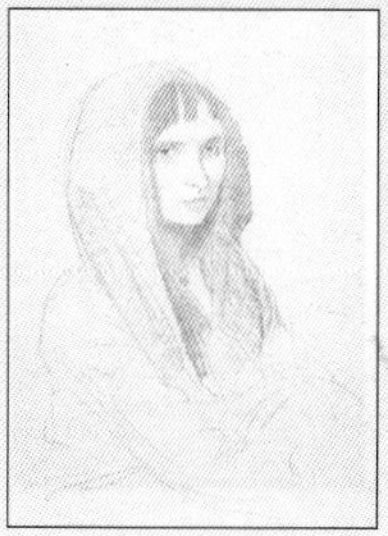

JOHN, Augustus
(1878-1961)

Dorelia McNeil as an Irish Girl, 1915-16

NMW A 1845
pastel on wove paper, 35.5 x 25.3
signed
Bequeathed by Margaret Davies, 1963

Provenance: Hugh Blaker; sold at The Leicester Galleries, March, 1937 (34) to Margaret Davies.

Bibliography: NMW, *Catalogue of the Margaret S. Davies Bequest of Paintings, Drawings and Sculpture*, Cardiff, 1963, p.42, no.129; M. Holroyd, *Augustus John - A Biography, vol.2, The Years of Experience*, London, 1975, pp.107-108 and 364-366; Augustus John, *Autobiography*, London, 1975, pp.107-108; M. Easton, M. Holroyd, *The Art of Augustus John*, London, 1976, pp.78-79 and 158-159; NMW, M. Evans, *Portraits by Augustus John, Family, Friends and the Famous*, Cardiff 1988, p.40, no.25.

Previously titled *An Irish Girl*.

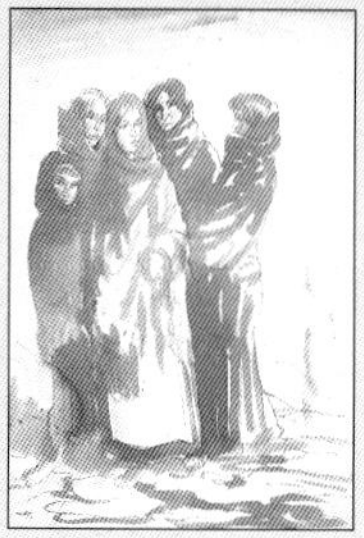

JOHN, Augustus
(1878-1961)

Galway Peasants

NMW A 3664
ink and wash (faded) on wove paper, 45.7 x 31.6
Bequeathed by Gwendoline Davies, 1952

Provenance: Chenil Galleries; purchased by Gwendoline Davies, December 1919.

Bibliography: NMW, *Catalogue of the Gwendoline E. Davies Bequest of Paintings, Drawings and Sculpture*, Cardiff, 1952, p.16, no.48; NMW, *Themes and Variations: the drawings of Augustus John*, Cardiff, 1996.

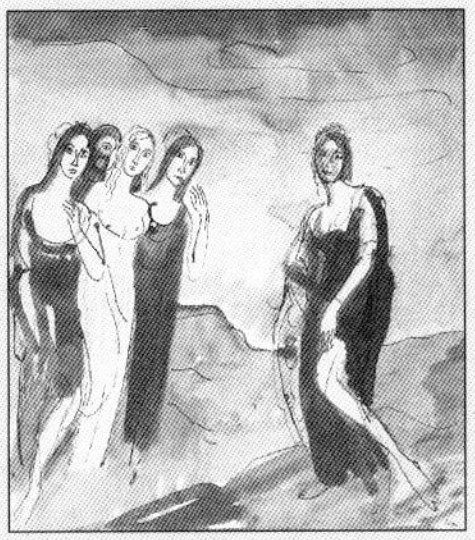

JOHN, Augustus
(1878-1961)

Group of Women

NMW A 14932
ink and wash on wove paper, 45.9 x 40.7
signed
Bequeathed by Gwendoline Davies, 1952

Provenance: Chenil Galleries; purchased by Gwendoline Davies, December 1919.

Bibliography: NMW, *Catalogue of the Gwendoline E. Davies Bequest of Paintings, Drawings and Sculpture*, Cardiff, 1952, p.16, no.52.

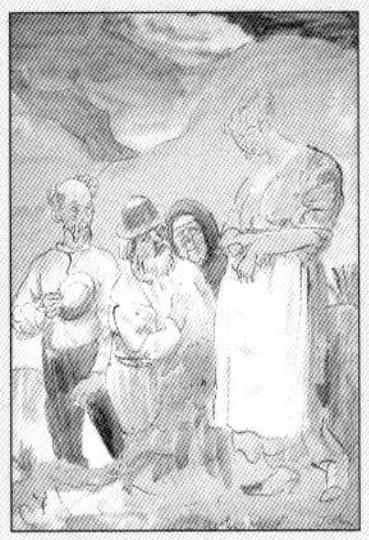

JOHN, Augustus
(1878-1961)

Irish Peasant's Courtship I

NMW A 14935
watercolour and oil based wash on wove paper, 50.9 x 35.6
signed
Bequeathed by Gwendoline Davies, 1952

Provenance: Chenil Galleries; purchased by Gwendoline Davies, December 1919.

Bibliography: NMW, *Catalogue of the Gwendoline E. Davies Bequest of Paintings, Drawings and Sculpture*, Cardiff, 1952, p.16, no.49.

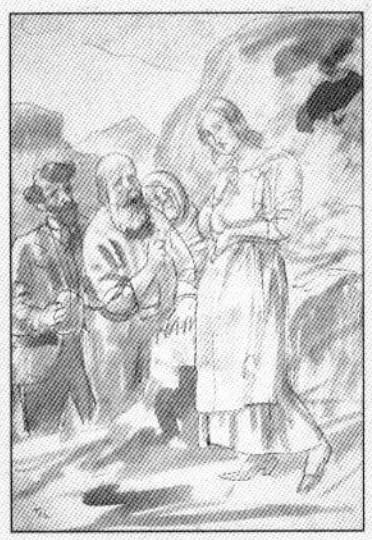

JOHN, Augustus
(1878-1961)

Irish Peasant's Courtship II

NMW A 14934
ink and wash on wove paper, 45.8 x 32.6
signed
Bequeathed by Gwendoline Davies, 1952

Provenance: Chenil Galleries; purchased by Gwendoline Davies, December 1919.

Bibliography: NMW, *Catalogue of the Gwendoline E. Davies Bequest of Paintings, Drawings and Sculpture*, Cardiff, 1952, p.16, no.50.

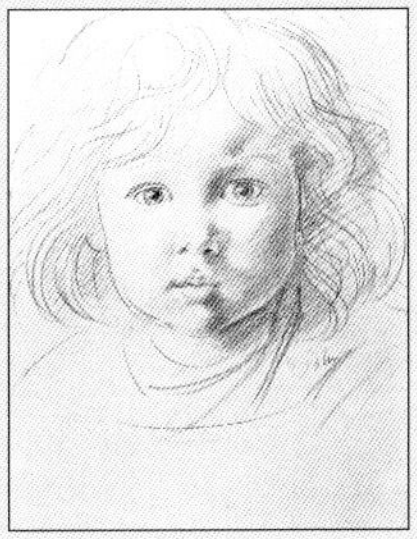

JOHN, Augustus
(1878-1961)

Pyramus John, 1908

NMW A 3225
pencil on wove paper, 35.5 x 25.3
signed
Bequeathed by Gwendoline Davies, 1952

Provenance: Chenil Galleries; purchased by Gwendoline Davies, December 1919.

Bibliography: NMW, *Catalogue of the Gwendoline E. Davies Bequest of Paintings, Drawings and Sculpture*, Cardiff, 1952, p.17, no.58; M. Holroyd, *Augustus John - A Biography, vol.1, The Years of Innocence*, London, 1974, pp.199-200; M. Holroyd, *Augustus John - A Biography, vol.2, The Years of Experience,* London, 1975, p.26; M. Easton, M. Holroyd, *The Art of Augustus John*, London, 1976, pp.68-9; M. Evans, *Portraits by Augustus John, Family, Friends and the Famous*, NMW Cardiff 1988, no.16, (illus) p.33.

Previously titled *Study of a Boy's Head*.

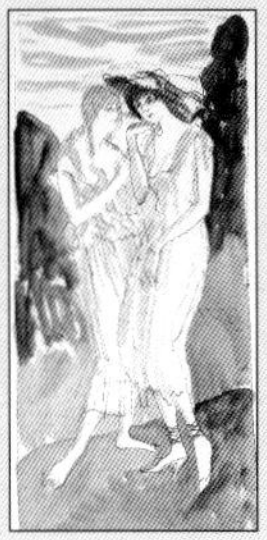

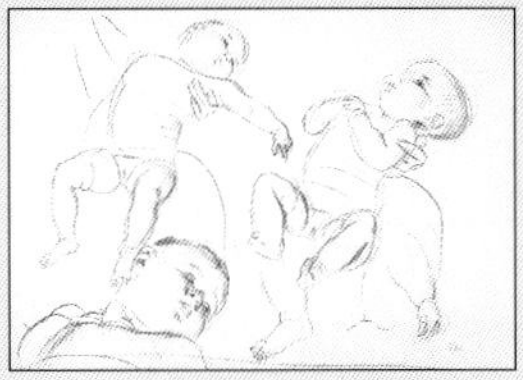

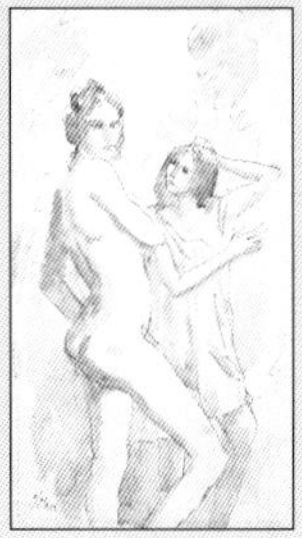

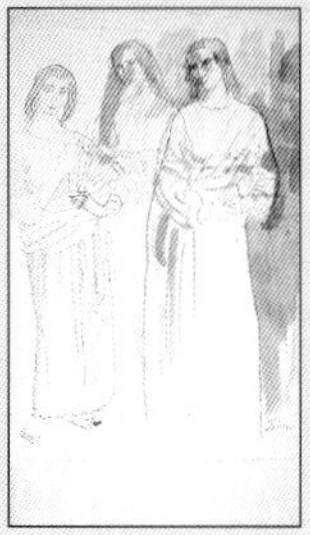

JOHN, Augustus
(1878-1961)

Secrets d'Amour

NMW A 14933
watercolour and ink on wove paper, 51 x 35.6
signed
Bequeathed by Gwendoline Davies, 1952

Provenance: Chenil Galleries; purchased by Gwendoline Davies, December 1919.

Bibliography: NMW, *Catalogue of the Gwendoline E. Davies Bequest of Paintings, Drawings and Sculpture*, Cardiff, 1952, p.17, no.54.

JOHN, Augustus
(1878-1961)

Studies of a Child

NMW A 14930
pencil on wove paper, 35.6 x 50.9
signed
Bequeathed by Gwendoline Davies, 1952

Provenance: Chenil Galleries; purchased by Gwendoline Davies, December 1919.

Bibliography: NMW, *Catalogue of the Gwendoline E. Davies Bequest of Paintings, Drawings and Sculpture*, Cardiff, 1952, p.17, no.57.

JOHN, Augustus
(1878-1961)

Study for 'The Bathers'

NMW A 14927
ink and wash on paper, 35.6 x 25.5
signed
Bequeathed by Gwendoline Davies, 1952

Provenance: Chenil Galleries; purchased by Gwendoline Davies, December 1919.

Bibliography: NMW, *Catalogue of the Gwendoline E. Davies Bequest of Paintings, Drawings and Sculpture*, Cardiff, 1952, p.16, no.51.

JOHN, Augustus
(1878-1961)

Three Women

NMW A 14928
ink and wash on wove paper, 46 x 26.8
signed
Bequeathed by Gwendoline Davies, 1952

Provenance: Chenil Galleries; purchased by Gwendoline Davies, December 1919.

Bibliography: NMW, *Catalogue of the Gwendoline E. Davies Bequest of Paintings, Drawings and Sculpture*, Cardiff, 1952, p.17, no.53.

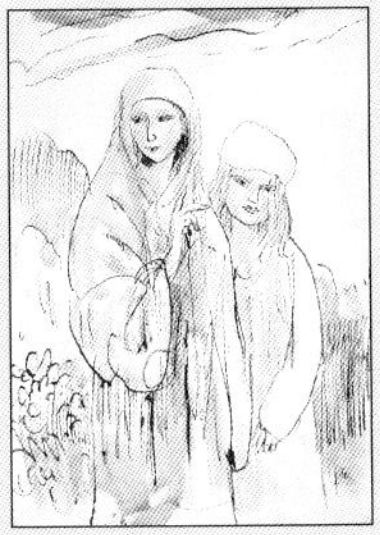

JOHN, Augustus
(1878-1961)

Wayfarers

NMW A 14929
ink and wash on wove paper, 35.8 x 25.4
signed
Bequeathed by Gwendoline Davies, 1952

Provenance: Chenil Galleries; purchased by Gwendoline Davies, December 1919.

Bibliography: NMW, *Catalogue of the Gwendoline E. Davies Bequest of Paintings, Drawings and Sculpture*, Cardiff, 1952, p.17, no.56.

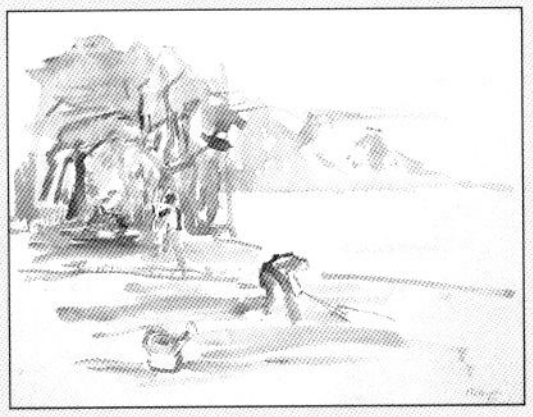

KOKOSCHKA, Oskar
(1886-1980)

Landscape with Bonfire, 1958

NMW A 1691
watercolour on Ingres paper, 47.7 x 63.4
signed and dated
Bequeathed by Margaret Davies, 1963

Provenance: Marlborough Fine Art Ltd, Kokoschka, Moore, Sutherland-watercolours and drawings, October 1962, (18); from where purchased by Margaret Davies for £700 on 12 November 1962.

Bibliography: Marlborough Fine Art Ltd., *Oskar Kokoschka in England and Scotland*, London, 1960, no.74; Marlborough Fine Art Ltd., *Watercolours and Drawings by Oskar Kokoschka, Henry Moore and Graham Sutherland*, London, 1962, no.18; NMW, *Catalogue of the Margaret S. Davies Bequest of Paintings, Drawings and Sculpture*, Cardiff, 1963, p.42, no.131

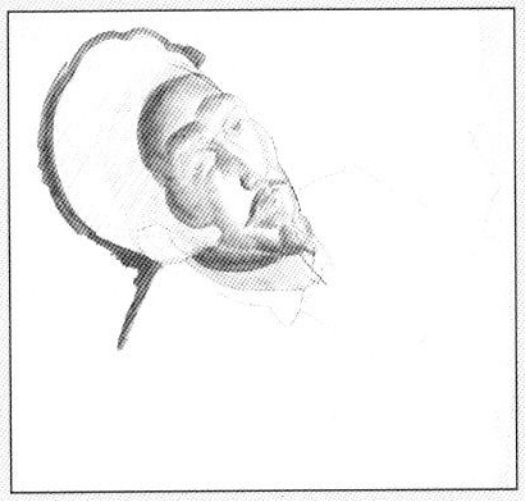

LEWIS, Percy Wyndham
(1882-1957)

Ezra Pound

NMW A 1867
pencil, watercolour and bodycolour on wove paper, 35.5 x 38.5
Bequeathed by Margaret Davies, 1963

Provenance: Leicester Galleries; from where purchased by Margaret Davies for £15-15-00, May 1921.

Bibliography: NMW, *Catalogue of the Margaret S. Davies Bequest of Paintings, Drawings and Sculpture*, Cardiff, 1963, p.43, no.132; W. Michel, *Wyndham Lewis*, London, 1971, no.347.

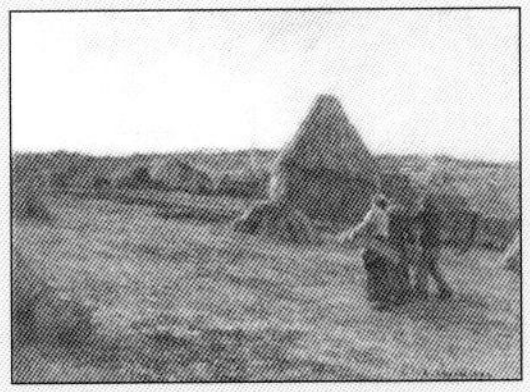

LHERMITTE, Léon Augustin
(1844-1925)

The Return of the Harvesters

NMW A 1692
pastel on buff paper over canvas, 35 x 45.1
signed
Bequeathed by Margaret Davies, 1963

Provenance: Boussod Valadon & Cie; from whom bought by Arthur Tooth & Sons; from whom bought by Margaret Davies, 4 July 1912, for £160.

Bibliography: NMW, *Catalogue of the Margaret S. Davies Bequest of Paintings, Drawings and Sculpture*, Cardiff, 1963, p.43, no.133; Monique le Pelley Fontenty, *Léon Augustin Lhermitte (1844-1925) Catalogue Raisonné*, Paris, 1991, p.191, no.170.

MARIS, Matthuis
(1839-1917)

Drapery Study, c.1874

NMW A 1686
pencil on wove paper, 14.9 x 23.8
verso: sketch of drapery
Bequeathed by Gwendoline Davies, 1952

Provenance: unknown, probably purchased from the French Gallery, 29 December 1913, at the same time as *He is Coming* (oil).

Bibliography: NMW, *Catalogue of the Gwendoline E. Davies Bequest of Paintings, Drawings and Sculpture*, Cardiff, 1952, p.19, no.66c.

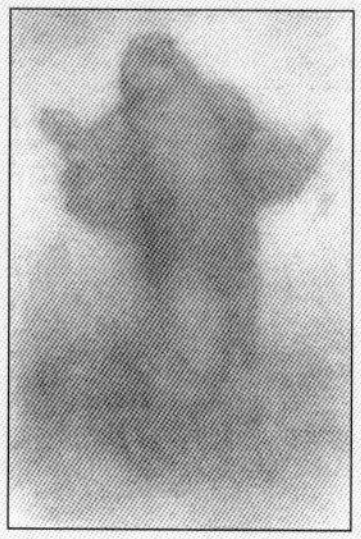

MARIS, Matthuis
(1839-1917)

Joyous Walk

NMW A 1687
crayon on wove paper, 29.8 x 20.6
Bequeathed by Gwendoline Davies, 1952

Provenance: W. Craibe Angus, Glasgow; D. Croal Thomson/French Gallery; from where sold to Gwendoline Davies on 28 November, 1913 with three other works: M. Maris, *In the Woods* (oil), H. Daumier, *Un Avocat* (oil), H. Daumier, *Dans la Rue* (oil), for a total of £1,800.

Bibliography: D. Croal Thompson, *Matthew Maris: A Souvenir*, London, 1918, no.31; NMW, *Catalogue of the Gwendoline E. Davies Bequest of Paintings, Drawings and Sculpture*, Cardiff, 1952, p.18, no.65; van Gelder, *Mattijs Maris*, Amsterdam, 1939, p.57.

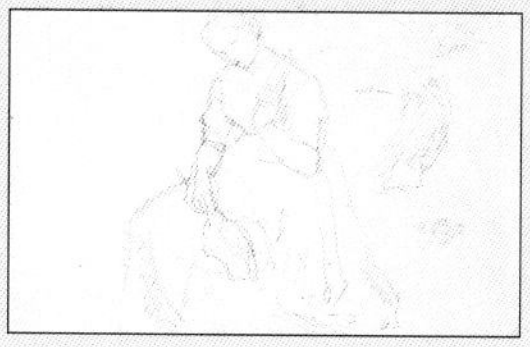

MARIS, Matthuis
(1839-1917)

Study of Seated Woman with Distaff, c.1874

NMW A 1684
pencil on wove paper, 14.9 x 23.9
verso: sketch of a cat, a baby, a lampshade and a hand
Bequeathed by Gwendoline Davies, 1952

Provenance: unknown, probably purchased from the French Gallery, 29 December 1913, at the same time as *He is Coming* (oil).

Bibliography: D. Croal Thompson, *Matthew Maris: A Souvenir*, London, 1918; NMW, *Catalogue of the Gwendoline E. Davies Bequest of Paintings, Drawings and Sculpture*, 1952, p.19, no.66b.

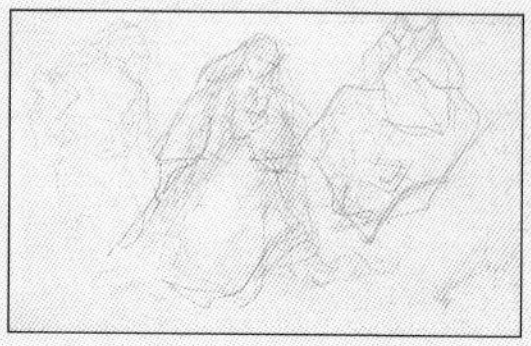

MARIS, Matthuis
(1839-1917)

Studies of a Seated Woman, c.1874

NMW A 1685
pencil on wove paper, 14.9 x 23.8
verso: sketch of drapery study, cats and hands
Bequeathed by Gwendoline Davies, 1952

Provenance: unknown, probably purchased from the French Gallery, 29 December 1913, at the same time as *He is Coming* (oil).

Bibliography: NMW, *Catalogue of the Gwendoline E. Davies Bequest of Paintings, Drawings and Sculpture*, Cardiff, 1952, p.19, no.66a.

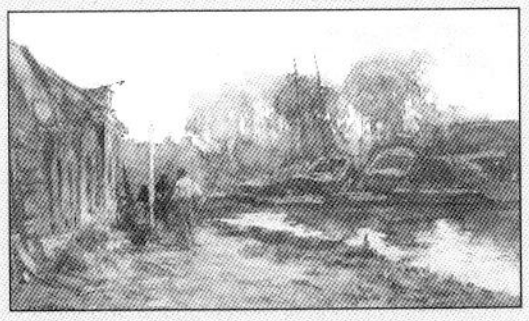

MASTENBROEK, Jan Hendrik van
(1875-1945)

Canal at Overschie, Setting Sun, 1899

NMW A 1693
watercolour, bodycolour and on wove paper, 18.6 x 32.2
signed and dated
Bequeathed by Margaret Davies, 1963

Provenance: Private collector Alexander Young; Thomas Agnew & Sons Gallery, London; bought by Margaret Davies for £32-0-0 on 28 February 1910.

Bibliography: NMW, *Catalogue of the Margaret S. Davies Bequest of Paintings, Drawings and Sculpture*, Cardiff, 1963, p.43, no.134.

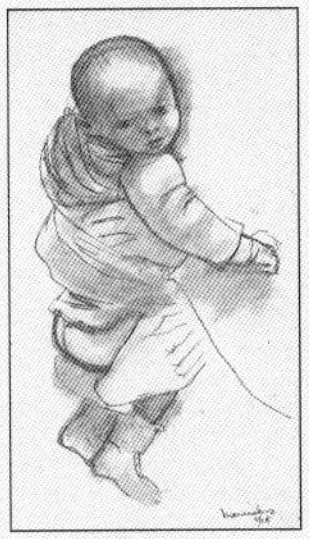

MENINSKY, Bernard
(1891-1950)

Baby in Arms, 1918

NMW A 1694
pen and ink and wash on wove paper, 24.1 x 13.9
signed and dated
Bequeathed by Margaret Davies, 1963

Provenance: Hugh Blaker; Jane Blaker by descent; The Leicester Galleries, London, *An exhibition of selected Paintings, Drawings and Sculpture from the Hugh Blaker collection* (49), sold to Margaret Davies, for £7-7-0 on March 1948.

Bibliography: Leicester Galleries, *Catalogue of an exhibition of selected Paintings, Drawings and Sculpture from the Hugh Blaker collection*, London, 1948, no.49; NMW, *Catalogue of the Margaret S. Davies Bequest of Paintings, Drawings and Sculpture*, Cardiff, 1963, p.44, no.135.

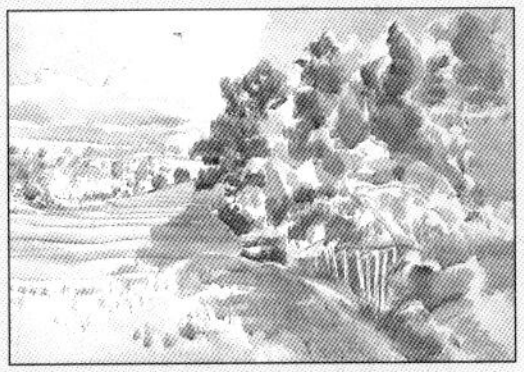

NASH, Paul
(1889 - 1946)

Field by the Wood, 1942

NMW A 1872
watercolour over pencil on wove paper, 39.6 x 57.5
signed
Bequeathed by Margaret Davies, 1963

Provenance: The Redfern Gallery; from where purchased by Margaret Davies on 9 June 1961 (321) for £350.

Bibliography: NMW, *Catalogue of the Margaret S. Davies Bequest of Paintings, Drawings and Sculpture*, Cardiff, 1963, p.44, no.136.

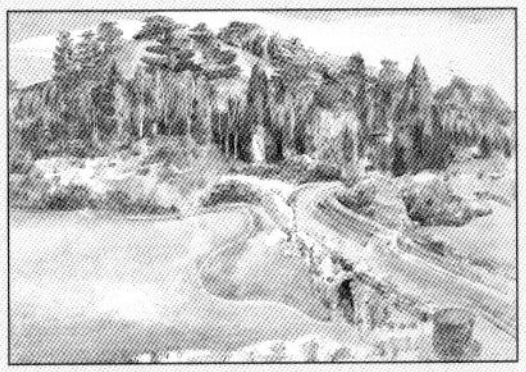

NASH, Paul
(1889 - 1946)

Gregynog, 1938

NMW A 1871
watercolour over pencil on wove paper, 39.8 x 57.6
signed
Bequeathed by Margaret Davies, 1963

Provenance: The Leicester Galleries; Guy H. Dixon; The Leicester Galleries; from whom purchased by Margaret Davies, March 1957 for £157.10

Bibliography: NMW, *Catalogue of the Margaret S. Davies Bequest of Paintings, Drawings and Sculpture*, Cardiff, 1963, p.44, no.137.

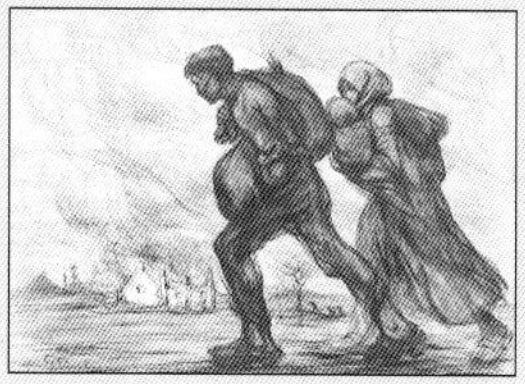

PAULUS, Pierre
(1881-1959)

The Flight, 1914

NMW A 1695
watercolour, crayon and pencil on wove paper, 25.1 x 35.3
signed and dated
Bequeathed by Margaret Davies, 1963

Provenance: unknown, probably purchased from the exhibition of Belgian art, Cardiff, 1915.

Bibliography: NMW, *Catalogue of the Margaret S. Davies Bequest of Paintings, Drawings and Sculpture*, Cardiff, 1963, p.44, no.138; M. Vincenteli, 'The Davies family and Belgian refugee artists and musicians in Wales', *The National Library of Wales Journal*, 22 (1981-82), pp.226-233.

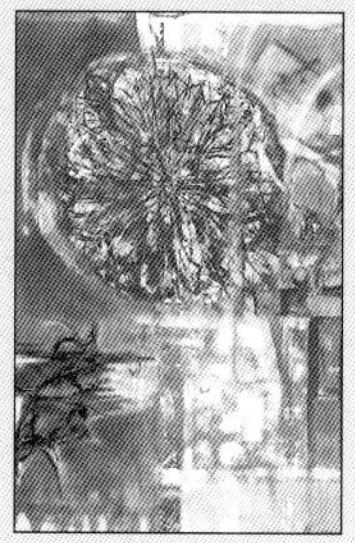

PHILIPSON, Robin, Sir
(1916-1992)

Rose Window

NMW A 14200
watercolour and ink on paper, 103.8 x 67.6
signed
Bequeathed by Margaret Davies, 1963

Provenance: Roland, Browse & Delbanco; from whom purchased by Margaret Davies on 29 October 1962 for £157.10.0.

Bibliography: NMW, *Catalogue of the Margaret S. Davies Bequest of Paintings, Drawings and Sculpture*, Cardiff, 1963, p.45, no.139.

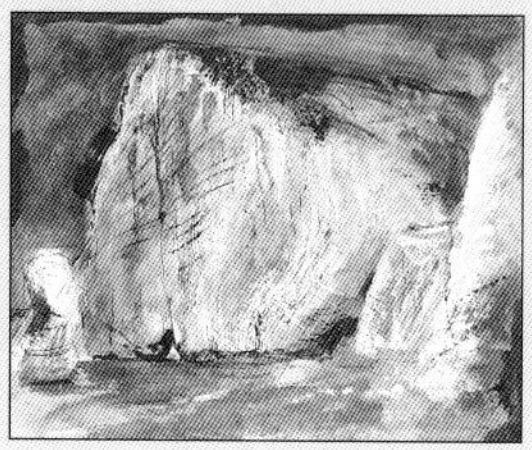

PIPER, John
(1903 - 1992)

Bats Head

NMW A 14117
watercolour, bodycolour, ink and pencil on paper, 53 x 65.5
signed
Bequeathed by Margaret Davies, 1963

Provenance: The Leicester Galleries, 1956; from whom purchased by Margaret Davies, 3 February 1956 for £85.5.0.

Bibliography: NMW, *Catalogue of the Margaret S. Davies Bequest of Paintings, Drawings and Sculpture*, Cardiff, 1963, p.45, no.140.

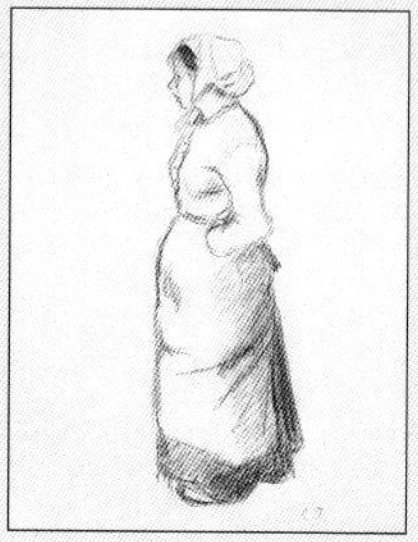

PISSARRO, Camille
(1831-1903)

Peasant Girl, c.1890

NMW A 1696
black chalk on blue wove paper, 39.5 x 31
signed with initials
Bequeathed by Margaret Davies, 1963

Provenance: The Leicester Galleries; sold to Margaret Davies from a Camille Pissarro exhibition, June 1920, no.45.

Bibliography: NMW, *Catalogue of the Margaret S. Davies Bequest of Paintings, Drawings and Sculpture*, Cardiff, 1963, p.45, no.141; NMW, J. Ingamells, *The Davies Collection of French Art*, Cardiff, 1967, p.72, pl.24b.

Previously titled *A Girl*.

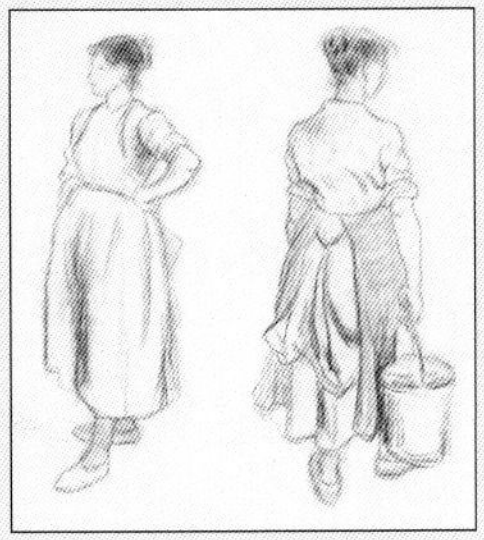

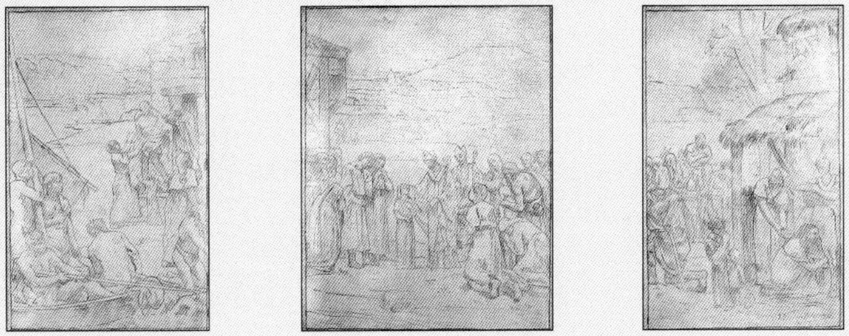

PISSARRO, Camille
(1831-1903)

Two Studies of a Girl, c.1890

NMW A 1697
chalk on pink laid paper, 47.9 x 62.5
watermark: A.L. in the centre of a symbol, ? a posthorn
Bequeathed by Margaret Davies, 1963

Provenance: The Leicester Galleries; sold to Margaret Davies from a Camille Pissarro exhibition, June 1920, no. 49.

Bibliography: NMW, *Catalogue of the Margaret S. Davies Bequest of Paintings, Drawings and Sculpture*, Cardiff, 1963, p.45, no.142; NMW, J. Ingamells, *The Davies Collection of French Art*, Cardiff, 1967, p.72, pl.24a; C. Lloyd, R. Thomson, *Impressionist Drawings from British Public and Private Collections*, 1986, no.60.

Previously titled *Two Girls*.

PUVIS DE CHAVANNES,
Pierre (1824-1898)

Study for 'Legende de Ste Geneviève', c.1875

NMW A 1698
ink on ground on canvas, 58.5 x 37.5(left panel), 58.2 x 46 (central panel), 58.3 x 37.4 (right panel)
Bequeathed by Margaret Davies, 1963

Provenance: M. Lepoutre; purchased by Bernheim-Jeune on 17 December 1919; from whom purchased by Margaret Davies, 12 March 1920 for Fr 15,000.

Bibliography: NMW, *Catalogue of the Margaret S. Davies Bequest of Paintings, Drawings and Sculpture*, Cardiff, 1963, p46, no.143; J. Ingamells, *The Davies Collection of French Art*, Cardiff, 1967, p.95 and p.l42; Arts Council of Great Britain, *French Symbolist Painters*, London, 1972, no.213.

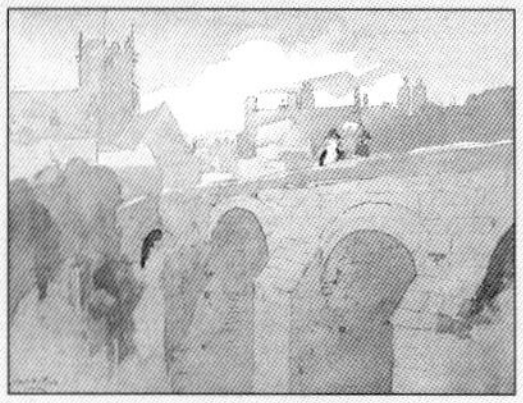

RICH, Alfred W.
(1856-1921)

Corfe

NMW A 16331
watercolour over pencil on wove paper,
28.3 x 37.7
signed
Bequeathed by Margaret Davies, 1963

Provenance: Walkers Galleries, April 1923 (99); from where purchased by Margaret Davies, 1923.

Bibliography: NMW, *Catalogue of the Margaret S. Davies Bequest of Paintings, Drawings and Sculpture*, Cardiff, 1963, p.47, no.147.

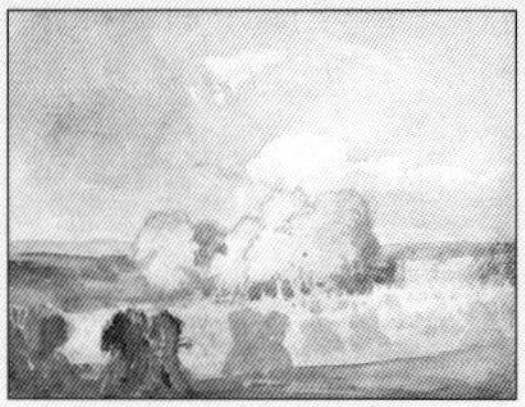

RICH, Alfred W.
(1856-1921)

Corn Stooks

NMW A 14920
watercolour over pencil on wove paper,
25.7 x 34.3
Bequeathed by Margaret Davies, 1963

Provenance: Walkers Galleries, April, 1923 (146), purchased by Margaret Davies, 1923.

Bibliography: NMW, *Catalogue of the Margaret S. Davies Bequest of Paintings, Drawings and Sculpture*, Cardiff, 1963, p.46, no.146.

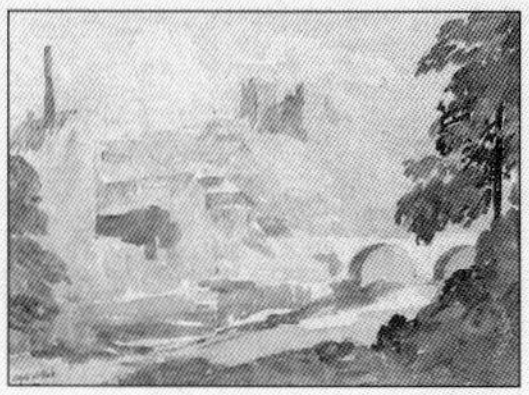

RICH, Alfred W.
(1856-1921)

Richmond, Yorkshire

NMW A 14939
watercolour over pencil on wove paper,
29.8 x 41.9
Bequeathed by Margaret Davies, 1963

Provenance: Walkers Galleries, April 1923 (109), purchased by Margaret Davies, 1923.

Bibliography: NMW, *Catalogue of the Margaret S. Davies Bequest of Paintings, Drawings and Sculpture*, Cardiff, 1963, p.46, no.144.

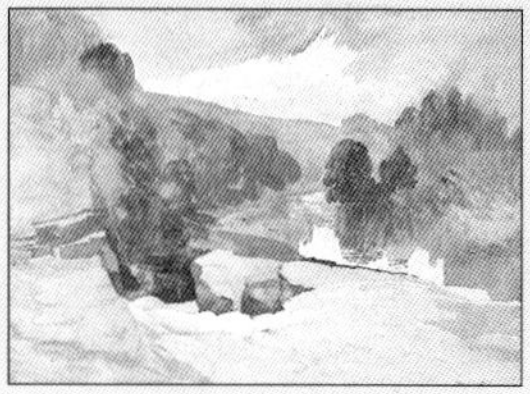

RICH, Alfred W.
(1856-1921)

The River at Ludlow

NMW A 14938
watercolour over pencil on wove paper,
35 x 47.6
Bequeathed by Margaret Davies, 1963

Provenance: Walkers Galleries, April 1923 (99); from where purchased by Margaret Davies, 1923.

Bibliography: NMW, *Catalogue of the Margaret S. Davies Bequest of Paintings, Drawings and Sculpture*, Cardiff, 1963, p.46, no.147.

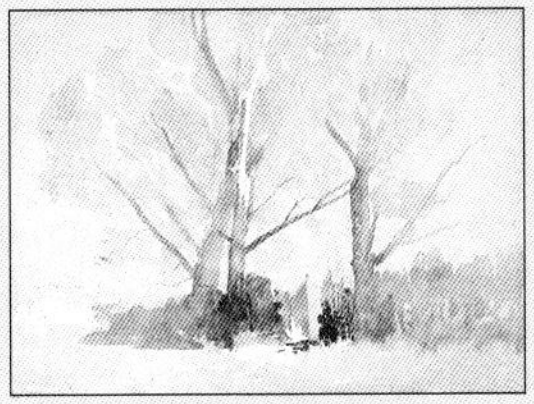

RICH, Alfred W.
(1856-1921)

Trees

NMW A 14936
watercolour over pencil on wove paper, 28.8 x 39.5
Bequeathed by Margaret Davies, 1963

Provenance: Walkers Galleries, April 1923 (247); from where purchased by Margaret Davies, 1923.

Bibliography: NMW, *Catalogue of the Margaret S. Davies Bequest of Paintings, Drawings and Sculpture*, Cardiff, 1963, p.46, no.145.

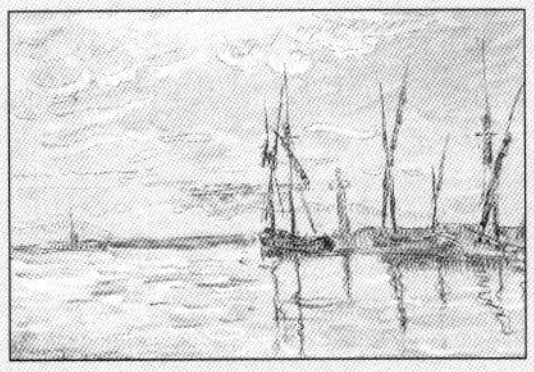

SIGNAC, Paul
(1863-1935)

St. Tropez, 1918

NMW A 1710
signed and dated
watercolour and crayon on wove paper, 27.1 x 40.7
Bequeathed by Gwendoline Davies, 1952

Provenance: Eldar Gallery, London, Exhibition no.10 (no.32 *Antibes*); from where purchased by Gwendoline Davies for £15-15-0 on 16 February 1920.

Bibliography: NMW, J. Ingamells, *The Davies Collection of French Art*, Cardiff, 1967, p.89, pl.39b.

Previously titled *Antibes.*

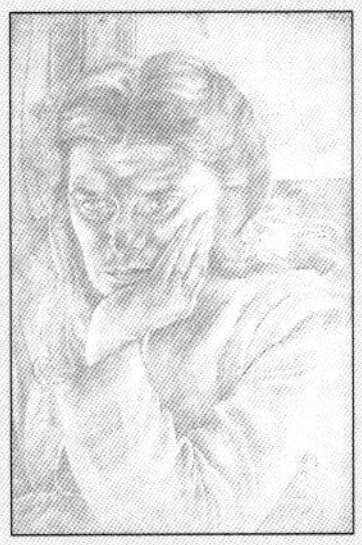

SPENCER, Stanley
(1891-1959)

Hilda Spencer, 1947

NMW A 14582
pencil on wove paper, 50.6 x 35.3
Bequeathed by Margaret Davies, 1963

Provenance: Dr. Eric Wilkes; Tooth & Sons Ltd, 1960; from where purchased by Margaret Davies for £150.0.0 on 7 September 1960.

Bibliography: NMW, Catalogue of the Margaret S. Davies bequest: *Paintings, Drawings and Sculpture*, Cardiff, 1963, p.47, no.149; Collis, *Stanley Spencer*, London 1962, p.88 and p.247;

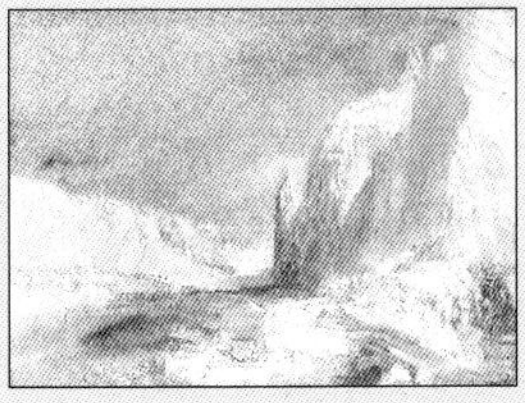

TURNER, Joseph Mallord William
(1775-1851)

Dinant

NMW A 1756
watercolour on blue wove paper, 13.9 x 19
Bequeathed by Gwendoline Davies, 1952

Provenance: John Edward Taylor; sold at Christie's sale on 5 July 1912 (lot 92), bought by Hugh Blaker on behalf of Gwendoline Davies, for £399.

Bibliography: NMW, *Catalogue of the Gwendoline E. Davies Bequest of Paintings, Drawings and Sculpture*, Cardiff, 1952, p.25, no.100; A. Wilton, *The Life & Work of J.M.W. Turner*, London, 1979, pp.421-2, no.1027; Tate Gallery, C. Powell, *Turner's Rivers of Europe: The Rhine, Meuse and Mosel*, London, 1991, p.162, no.100.

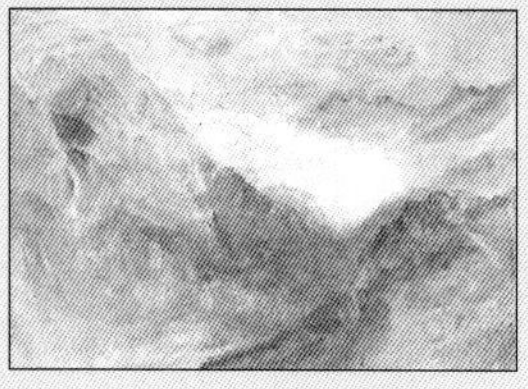

TURNER, Joseph Mallord William (1775-1851)

Fort de L'Esseillon, Val de la Maurienne, c.1835

NMW A 1744
watercolour on wove paper, 24.2 x 34.8
Bequeathed by Gwendoline Davies, 1952

Provenance: Wallis & Son/The French Gallery; from where bought by Gwendoline Davies for £130, 28 in November 1913.

Bibliography: NMW, *Catalogue of the Gwendoline E. Davies Bequest of Paintings, Drawings and Sculpture*, Cardiff, 1952, p.25, no.97; A. Wilton, *The Life & Work of J.M.W. Turner*, London, 1979, no.1431.

Comments: Previously titled *Swiss Mountains*. Re-identified by David Hill.

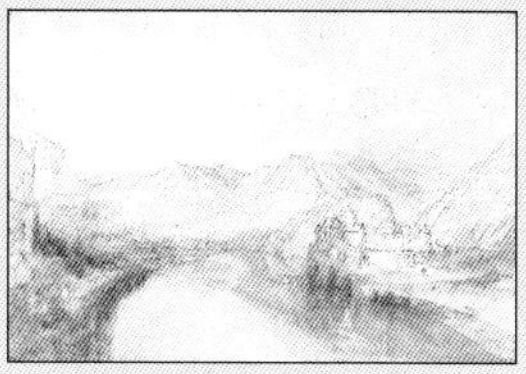

TURNER, Joseph Mallord William (1775-1851)

The Mouse Tower

NMW A 1740
watercolour over pencil on wove paper, 17.5 x 23.8
verso: pencil sketch of leaning tower
Bequeathed by Gwendoline Davies, 1952

Provenance: unknown, purchased by Gwedoline Davies between 1908 and 1927.

Bibliography: NMW, *Catalogue of the Gwendoline E. Davies Bequest of Paintings, Drawings and Sculpture*, Cardiff, 1952, p.26, no.101; A. Wilton, *The Life & Work of J.M.W. Turner*, London, 1979, no.1346; Whitechapel Art Gallery, *J.M.W. Turner R.A. 1775-1851*, London, 1953.

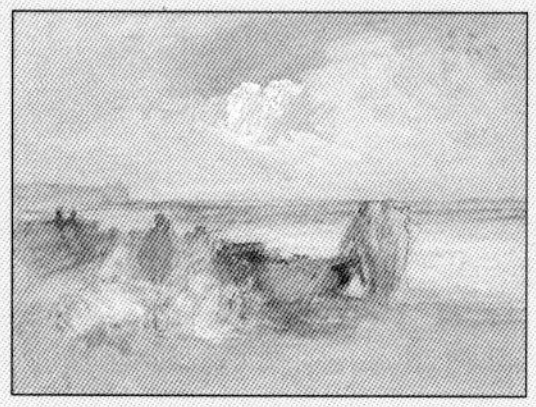

TURNER, Joseph Mallord William (1775-1851)

Margate

NMW A 1745
watercolour and chalk on blue wove paper, 14 x 18.9
Bequeathed by Gwendoline Davies, 1952

Provenance: Hugh Blaker; D. Croal Thompson; probably purchased by Gwendoline Davies in 1919, although there are no records of this transaction.

Bibliography: NMW, *Catalogue of the Gwendoline E. Davies Bequest of Paintings, Drawings and Sculpture*, Cardiff, 1952, p.25, no.94; Whitechapel Art Gallery, *J.M.W. Turner R.A. 1775-1851*, London, 1953, no.224; A. Wilton, *The Life & Work of J.M.W. Turner*, London, 1979, no.920.

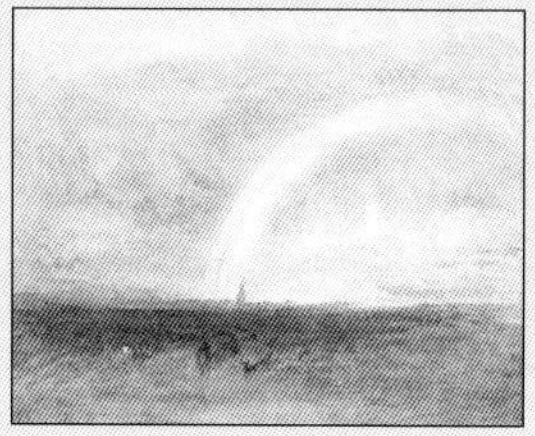

TURNER, Joseph Mallord William (1775-1851)

The Rainbow

NMW A 1743
watercolour on wove paper, 23.9 x 30.0
Bequeathed by Gwendoline Davies, 1952

Provenance: John Edward Taylor; sold at Christie's 5 July 1912 (85) to Thomas Agnew and Son for £609; sold to J.F. Haworth; sold back to Thomas Angew and Son in November 1918; sold to D. Croal Thompson; from where purchased by Gwendoline Davies, 12 July 1919, for £800.

Bibliography: NMW, *Catalogue of the Gwendoline E. Davies Bequest of Paintings, Drawings and Sculpture*, Cardiff, 1952, p.25, no.98; J.T.H. Bailey (ed), 'The Taylor Collection', *The Connoisseur*, 34 (1912), pp.29-37.

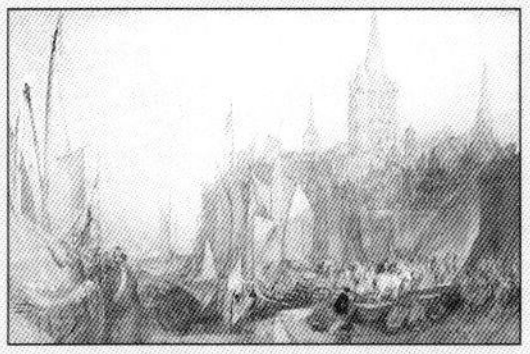

TURNER, Joseph Mallord William (1775-1851)

Rhine Gate, Cologne, 1819

NMW A 1755
watercolour with scratching out on paper on board, 19.9 x 30.8
Bequeathed by Gwendoline Davies, 1952

Provenance: Walter Fawkes; by descent to Rev. Ayscough Fawkes (verso inscribed from the Farnley Hall Collection); sold at Christie's, 27 June 1890 (34), to D.P.McEuen for £147; sold at Christie's, 1 April 1911 (79), to Eaton; Charles McEuen; sold at Christie's 2 August 1918 (84), to Hugh Blaker for £152-5-0; D Croal Thomson, Barbizon House; from where purchased by Gwendoline Davies for £350, 19 July 1919

Bibliography: NMW, *Catalogue of the Gwendoline E. Davies Bequest of Paintings, Drawings and Sculpture*, Cardiff, 1952, p.25, no.96; A. Wilton, *The Life & Work of J.M.W. Turner*, London, 1979, no.669; Wallraf-Richartz-Museum, Cologne, *J.M. William Turner Koln und der Rhein*, no.4.

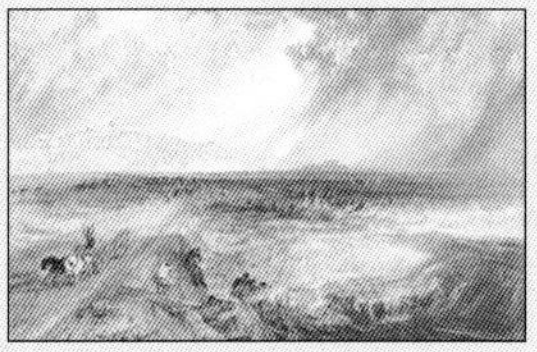

TURNER, Joseph Mallord William (1775-1851)

Rye, Sussex, 1824

NMW A 1742
watercolour with scraping out on wove paper, 14.8 x 23.1
watermark: J Whatman/Turkey Mills 1819
Bequeathed by Gwendoline Davies, 1952

Provenance: Charles Birch by 1834 (lent to exhibition of Royal Birmingham Society of Artists); John Miller 1858; sold at Christie's 20 May 1858 to Farrer; Matthew Uzielli; sold at Christie's 12 April 1861 (236) to Mason; C. Sackville Bale; sold at Christie's 14 May 1881 (194) to Vokins for £357-0-0; S.G. Holland by 1886; sold at Christie's 25 June 1908 (262) to Hugh Blaker on behalf of Gwendoline Davies for £682-10-0.

Bibliography: C.F. Bell, *A list of works contributed to public exhibitions by J.M.W. Turner*, London, 1901, p.169; NMW, *Catalogue of the Gwendoline E. Davies Bequest of Paintings, Drawings and Sculpture*, Cardiff, 1952, p.25, no.99; A. Wilton, *The Life & Work of J.M.W. Turner*, London, 1979, no.471; Eric Shanes, *Turner in 1066 Country exhibition catalogue*, 1998 (Hastings Art Gallery), no. 43, (illus) p.7.

Comments: Drawing of this view is in the Hastings Sketchbook (TB CXXXIX - 21v, 22); Edward Goodall, engraved this view for *Southern Coast*, vol.1, pl.17.

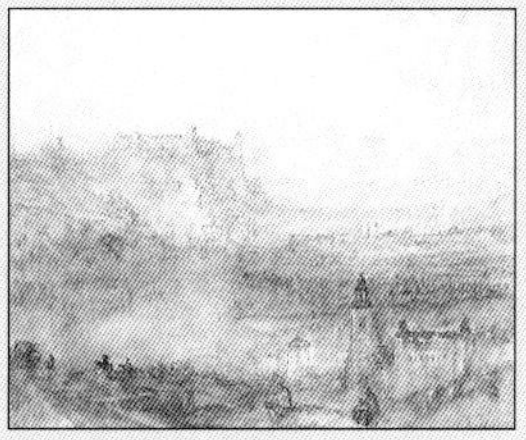

TURNER, Joseph Mallord William (1775-1851)

Würzburg

NMW A 1753
watercolour on wove paper, 23.1 x 28.8
Bequeathed by Gwendoline Davies, 1952

Provenance: John Edward Taylor; sold at Christie's 5 July 1912 (56) to Thomas Agnew & Son for £1312-10-0; D. Croal Thomson at Barbizon House; from whom purchased by Gwendoline Davies on 12 July 1919 for £1520-0-0.

Bibliography: J.T.H. Bailey (ed), 'The Taylor collection', *The Connoisseur*, 34 (1912), pp.29-37, p.36; NMW, *Catalogue of the Gwendoline E. Davies Bequest of Paintings, Drawings and Sculpture*, Cardiff, 1952, p.25, no.95; Whitechapel Art Gallery, *J.M.W. Turner R.A. 1775-1851*, London, 1953, no.216; A. Wilton, *The Life & Work of J.M.W. Turner*, London, 1979, no.1322; Wallraf-Richartz-Museum, Cologne, *J.M. William Turner Koln und der Rhein*, no.61.

Previously titled *Ehrenbreitstein* and *Coblenz*.

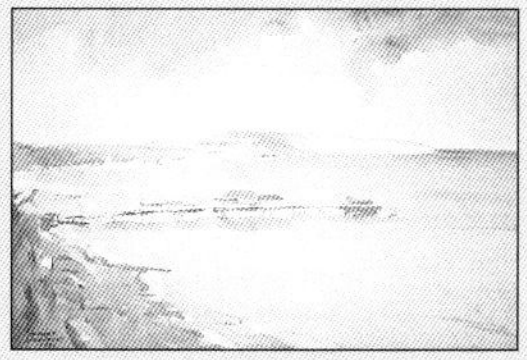

URQUHART, Murray (1880-1972)

Shanklin, 1904

NMW A 14585
watercolour and bodycolour on wove paper, 34 x 54.2
signed and dated
watermark: verso: FIDELIS
Bequeathed by Margaret Davies, 1963

Provenance: unknown, acquired by Margaret Davies by 1962.

Bibliography: NMW, *Catalogue of the Margaret S. Davies Bequest of Paintings, Drawings and Sculpture*, Cardiff, 1963, p.47, no.150.